BY YOUR SIDE

By
HOW TO FIND
Your
SOULFUL ALLIES &
Side
BECOME ONE TO OTHERS

David Richo

SHAMBHALA

Shambhala Publications, Inc.
2129 13th Street
Boulder, Colorado 80302
www.shambhala.com

Cover design: Amanda Weiss
Interior design: Kate Huber-Parker

9 8 7 6 5 4 3 2 1

First Edition
Printed in the United States of America

Shambhala Publications makes every
effort to print on acid-free, recycled paper.
Shambhala Publications is distributed worldwide by
Penguin Random House, Inc., and its subsidiaries.

Library of Congress Cataloging-in-Publication Data
Names: Richo, David, 1940– author.
Title: By your side: how to find soulful allies and become one to others /
    David Richo.
Identifiers: LCCN 2023048128 | ISBN 9781645473053 (trade paperback)
Subjects: LCSH: Friendship. | Fellowship. | Allyship.
Classification: LCC BF575.F66 R54 2024 | DDC 177/.62—dc23/eng/20231106
LC record available at https://lccn.loc.gov/2023048128

To my grandson Nicholas, age two:

I am always accompanying you
and may you always be an assisting force
to this floating world.

CONTENTS

BY YOUR SIDE

INTRODUCTION

We're all in this together.

—Matthew Gerrard and Robbie Nevil,
High School Musical

We have all heard expressions along the lines of the following:

She is there (or here) for me.
He comes through for me.
They are in my corner.
He is on my team.
She supports me.
He has my back.
They prop me up.
They encourage the best in me.
She backs me up.
He stands up for me (or stands by me).
She believes in me.
They are at my side, by my side.
He has my best interests at heart.
She shows me who I am.
They look out for me, step in when needed.
He helps me be myself.
She is someone I can always turn to.

I can always count on them.
He says and means, "I got you."
She stays with me through thick and thin.
We are joined at the hip.

These are references to a necessary and needed character on our human journey: the ally, the reliable companion, the assisting force. And, of course, these are all other names for love, what we so much need, the implicit subject of this entire book. Indeed, the challenge to be human is a group project. We were born with the full spectrum of human capacities but we can only activate them with assistance from others. We have bodies that can walk but someone has to show us how. We have language ability but we can only use it by hearing others speak. We were born with unique talents, all in bud. Only with the patient and encouraging help of others can those talents blossom. In other words, we can't be human unless others assist us along the way. It takes a buddy for a bud to bloom. Others buddy up to us and we do the same for them. We need one another to become fully human.

The term "assisting force" usually refers to a specific character in tales the world over and all through the centuries. In every heroic journey story the hero or heroine requires a steadfast comrade to rely on for assistance—a metaphor for how our own personal fulfillment necessitates the assistance of others. The assisting force is someone (or more than one person) who steps in to help, who lends a hand or a heart or a shoulder, who acts on our behalf.

An assisting force accompanies, guides, guards, informs, prompts, and collaborates with us on our life journey. This ally energy is commonly personified in stories and films as a best friend, a sidekick, an aide, a wise old man or woman who serves as an adviser, a pathfinder, a partner, a spirit guide. Even the so-called "Lone" Ranger has Tonto, the famously stereotypical "trusty Indian companion," to help him. The moment always comes when the strong person, the assisting force to others, needs someone *else* no matter how strong she may be. The fact that no one has ever trod the whole path without help reflects the very nature of humans as social animals—that is, as interdependent. A sense of belonging is primary in our consciousness and necessary for our survival. We feel its welcome at birth into a family, at school, among peers, in a religious affiliation, at work, in our loyalty to a home team. We feel it also and wonderfully in nature as we find our place under a tree. In fact, since everything in nature is connected to everything else, everything in nature is an assisting force. Assistance flows from connection.

We have seen Western films in which a general asks another general for reinforcements. We have also heard the words "the cavalry is coming"—that is, help is on the way. These are examples of how helping forces step in to meet the needs of others, helping them complete a task, the help we all need sometimes. "Help on the way" can mean not only that help is coming in response to an immediate need but also that help is needed on our way through life.

The word "helper" may give the impression that someone has what we don't have. That can be true but it does not apply to the archetype of an assisting force. Since the main assisting force is within us, others activate what we already have. *Assisting forces reflect inner resources.* So our topic in this book is not dualistic—a denial of our wholeness but unitary—an affirmation of it. True alliance is about sharing in kinship, not top-down helping. Our topic is accompaniment, the ever-shimmering, ever-cherished gift that one human being can offer to another.

INSTEAD OF ISOLATION

The necessary ingredient of accompaniment shows us why *abandonment* is our worst fear. Being left by all who were there for us before—alone with no one to turn to, left out—will scare us as a fate worse than death. Actually, it *is* death, since life for humans can only proceed successfully as a life together. Some of us were abandoned in childhood, some in adulthood, some in both. That was not simply a loss of a presence that mattered. That was terrifying trauma, inflicting a wound that takes a lifetime to heal. Our focus in this book is on the idea of assisting forces not as add-ons but as essential ingredients of safety and security, what we need and always needed to survive. Now we see why being abandoned or excluded by other people is so terrifying. We live by inclusion, by our guarantees of acceptance and worthiness and the self-esteem they generate.

The despair and lonesomeness that so many people feel these days may be healed by opening to the assisting forces, visible and invisible, that end human isolation. In our world today we witness so much breakdown of community. Only human solidarity, alliance, can make a difference if we are to survive. Sartre's famous phrase "Hell is other people" can then resplendently change to "Hell happens when there are no other people."

Every one of us will need support from others throughout our lifespan, no matter how powerful, self-sufficient, or wise we may be. Too often, we plod along, believing we can go it alone, forgetting—or never noticing—that so many allies, with so many graces, have joined us and await their chance to be there for us. This lack of awareness is why a person with an inflated ego—which thinks it needs no one—loses so much and is ultimately so spiritually impoverished. The go-it-alone self is, ironically, a self-contraction. We will keep finding out just how fragile and feeble are the powers of such a grandiose, though hobbled, ego. Indeed, one of the saddest of human predicaments is acting as if safety and security were only possible when we maintain staunch individualism. Then we are trusting division rather than togetherness, illusion rather than reality. In fact, as we shall see in this book, it is a disability to be unable or unwilling to ask for help throughout our lifespan—especially in old age.

What works best on this pot-holed terrain called life is synergy, joining forces with our allies every step of the way. Now we see why it hurts so much to be rejected by others, especially family members, made to feel like an outsider, boycotted. Not to be in the right clique in high school or be included in the group at work that goes out for a beer together can easily wound our self-esteem. Indeed, since we mammals only thrive in a group or family, expulsion is ultimately the equivalent of death. The "lone" wolf in fact can only survive in a pack that includes him. We see again how abandonment is the central fear in all mammals and how accompaniment the central comfort.

It is the joy of connectedness that alerts us to our longing for a wider domain than that of our own identity. Indeed, clinging to a separate isolated sense of self is a cause of suffering; we have cut our hearts in half. In all-embracing relatedness we see at last the farther reaches of ourselves, too vast for one name or one body or even one country.

A recognition of the importance of assisting forces may even underlie our fascination in recent years with the attachment theory in psychology. In spiritual consciousness, the theory can take on a wider significance. A secure attachment does not have to be limited to early family bonds; in spiritual maturation it can extend to include all beings. Then our developmental task of autonomy and connection becomes easier. Our goal is independence within interdependence—what the web of life has been about all along.

WHAT IS AN ALLY?

The word "ally" has gained modern parlance to indicate a person who is not a member of a marginalized or mistreated group but who expresses or gives support to that group. But in this book, we will be using the term in its original definition, to indicate any trustworthy helper—an associate who supports, fortifies, and assists us.

Here are some examples of what assisting forces might look like:

- Someone who cares about us and is willing to be our go-to
- A wise guide
- A supporter of our growth and evolution
- A companion who does not fail us
- A protector or backer
- A cheerleader who both alerts us to and fosters our inner strengths and talents
- Someone who gives us a sense of inclusion and belonging no matter what
- Someone who really gets us—that is, attunes to our feelings, needs, and longings
- Someone who says just the right thing at the right time and it makes a positive impact on us
- Someone who is not afraid to confront us on our mistakes, inadequacies, and addictions—but always in a way that supports what is best for us
- Someone who helps us stabilize ourselves when we have a breakdown or hit bottom
- Someone who pinch-hits for us until we can show up again
- Someone with whom there are ties that transcend time and distance, ties that can't be severed by changes in circumstances, distance, or even death

Any person, experience, or thing that offers one or more of these benefits is a personal assisting force, an ally. All our allies together form what we call a support system. Since assisting forces are necessary for life to be rich and full, our cherishing and expanding our circle of friends and supporters is necessary too. We only survive and thrive accompanied.

We are also essential to the circle of assisting forces surrounding our friends. Our coming through for others is necessary for their happiness and is a practice of love on our part. Or another way of saying it is: assisting forces are links of love from others to us and from us to others. Friendship is a central and most touching way for that love to be displayed. Alliance is ultimately the glue of the human family. Carl Sagan, in *Contact*, wrote: "In all our searching, the only thing we've found that makes all the emptiness bearable is each other."

We are also surrounded by societal or group-specific assisting forces. For instance, lawmakers and judges are allies of our society when they take a stand for democracy, ecology, and human rights. They act as assisting forces when they take a stand against prejudice and exclusion, working to protect freedom, equality, and survival. Spurred on by their courage we too may feel a calling to be assisting forces in our world. This will be more than just imitation. They are showing us our purpose in the human family, to be allies to one another, both personally and societally. All it takes is courage, a sterling characteristic of all assisting forces.

WE CAN'T MAKE IT ALONE

"Ally" means "connection," as we see in its Latin root, *alligare*, "bind to." The word "companion" literally means "one who shares bread (Latin: *panis*) with us." Indeed, our circle of allies is present with us at life's banquet. We are celebrating the feast of our full humanness and our victory over the darkness of isolation. After all, "connection," in its deepest sense, means "intimacy."

None of this is new. We have always known we do not find our way alone. We know we are supported by a long line of people who have helped us on life's winding ways. As we look back over the choices and events of our lives we realize that almost every one of them was sparked by someone else. A word, an encouragement, a dare, a recommendation, an example moved us to give something a try that we might never have ventured on our own. We *needed* a push from an assisting force to move into finding out what we really wanted, what we were really good at, who we really are. (We know what we really want only when we are doing all it takes to get it—including asking for help!)

Indeed, we humans survive abundantly only because we live in a guild of artisans of humanness. From the very beginning of life we are in the hands of knowledgeable others, relying on them for survival and growth. Indeed, we arrived in the world in the midst of such allies. Our parents gave us life, someone delivered us at birth, family and the world around us came through in ways that fostered our maturation. Indeed, because of so much companionship, seen and unseen, we can even say there is no such thing as aloneness. Nor are there dividing lines between us—only connections we feel or fail to notice.

Once we are aware of so much helpful companionship in our lives we might ask: What makes people want to be assisting forces to one another? The answer highlights the most beautiful characteristic of our humanity: love. Part of loving others is caring about them and for them, being their allies, helping them grow into the best they can be, standing beside them as they face what life presents to them. Likewise, we may feel it is our calling to be helpers, to give ourselves to being of service—another reason we may become assisting forces. All in all, we see that our topic in this book originates, expresses itself, and leads to the blossoming of love. Could there be a more wonderful theme to explore?

The word "mammal" is from the Latin for "breast," our source of survival as infants. From the earliest moments of life we also needed mirroring—that is, our parents' or caretakers' recognition of and reflection back to us of our needs and feelings. A loving parent identifies a child's needs to be nursed or held and fulfills those needs warmly and willingly. This experience repeated multiple times is the origin of trust. It also creates positive reinforcement as we name our needs and make bids for their fulfillment—both in early life and beyond. Since we will always have needs, we will be seeking ongoing validation of our feelings from others. In relationships we will also seek allies who mirror our deepest needs, values, and wishes. We will always be seeking affirmation of who we are, as we are. That need began in childhood and carries forward into our adult relationships.

This beautiful statement from the Jewish existentialist Martin Buber in his 1951 essay "Distance and Relation" perfectly describes our ineradicable need for affirmation: "A person wishes to be confirmed in his being by another person . . . Secretly and bashfully, he watches for a Yes which allows him to be and which can come only from one human person to another. It is from one human being to another that the heavenly bread of self-being is passed." I find more depth in these words with every passing year, especially as, one by one, so many of my cherished family members and friends are passing from this floating world. And, yes, the memories of them abide, assist, and soothe.

What about help from our loved ones who have died? Some of us believe we came from nothing and go back to nothing. Some of us believe we came from everything and go back to everything. If we believe in an afterlife we might also sometimes feel we are receiving help from those who have loved us but have passed away. Then their death is not simply their reabsorption into the earth; it is a passage into a new form of being an ally of humanity. Bodies die but bonds don't. We may still feel accompanied by our now-gone companions, especially at critical times in life. The ongoing caring we may feel from the dead represents a trust that compassion endures beyond death. Elizabeth Barrett Browning expresses this enduring bond in Sonnet 43, to her husband:"How do I love thee? . . . I shall but love thee better after death."

Indeed, both in Buddhism and in religious faith those of us who are here on earth and those who have died all form a single human community. In Buddhism this is the work of bodhisattvas, enlightened beings who keep helping us. In Christian theology it is called the "communion of saints." We will discuss both of these concepts later in this book.

CHALLENGED BY AFFLICTION

An assisting force is a backer. The opposite of someone backing us up is someone putting us down—thwarting our intents, hindering our progress, sabotaging our growth. We have all met people like that. They are not assisting forces but *afflicting* forces. In any heroic journey story the hero or heroine meets up with both assisting and afflicting characters. For instance, Iago is an afflictive character in Shakespeare's *Othello*. He poisons Othello's mind against his loving wife and this ends in bloodshed, just what Iago wanted to have happen. In the film *The Wizard of Oz*, Dorothy's three friends and Glinda the good witch are assisting forces while the evil witch and her army are afflicting forces. As we know, ultimately both forces helped Dorothy find her own power. The Irish-born politician Edmund Burke expressed this paradox in his *Reflections on the Revolution in France* (1790): "He that wrestles with us strengthens our nerves, and sharpens our skill. Our antagonist is our helper." A parallel Buddhist idea from the *Bodhicaryavatara* (*The Way of the Bodhisattva*) shows us the spiritual possibility, the path to virtue: "I delight in my enemy since he is a companion on my path to enlightenment. He is the cause of patience."

Bodhisattvas and saints sometimes comfort us with a kindly pat—but at other times they challenge us with a Zen blow that cuts through our ego-sheltering delusions. This blow is not an afflicting force but an assisting one. All true allies serve to provide the initiatory process into full adulthood that we all need, so their impact on us may indeed prove painful—as all initiations are. For instance, sometimes allies give our self-centered ego a comeuppance so that our true other-loving self can emerge. What is meant to assist may also feel like it afflicts. Wisdom is knowing the difference. Heroism is welcoming both—appreciating one and growing from our encounter with the other.

MORE THAN VISIBLE

The assisting forces in our lives are not limited to people who help us. Our allies are visible and invisible, tangible and intangible, seen and unseen, known and unknown. This combination also appears in stories. Even if there is no one showing up in the flesh, the hero or heroine can turn to a transcendent god, Buddha, or the universe—some power from beyond the material world. Spiritual assisting forces in stories and in life are metaphors for a companionship that goes beyond what the eye can see.

Ultimately, the archetype of the assisting force, the visible or invisible ally who shows up just in time, gives us an assurance that we are not alone. As the American poet Emily Dickinson asserted: "Alone, I cannot be— For Hosts do visit me." Similarly, the Argentine writer Jorge Luis Borges observed on the task of art: "You think you are alone, and as the years go by, if the stars are on your side, you may discover that you are at the center of a vast circle of invisible friends whom you will never get to know but who love you. And that is an immense reward." In their work, both of these wise advisors are reminding us that we are not beings but cobeings. We are not like Gibraltar; we are like deer and dahlias, unable to make it alone. Every being, especially we humans, exists and endures only in a web of trusted kinship. This book is about how that happens, how it can happen more effectively, how it leads us to an immensely fruitful spiritual practice.

I am thankful to the many authors whose work and research I refer to in this book. As with all my books, this one is not meant to be science but distillation, the fruit of my experience, learning, and contemplation. And I love having this chance to share it all with you—I deeply appreciate my chance to be an assisting force.

In what follows you will find yourself remembering and visiting many early and recent companions. They are the ones who stayed with you through thick and thin, who escorted you into new rooms in your own inner world, who showed you a walkway in the wilderness.

You will see how not only people but animals, things, and all of nature stayed with you too.

You will see that what you held dear has, in so many ways, reliably sustained you—and sustains you still, in cherished memories.

And most of all, you will find out how you are, already and always, the companion ally of so many whose lives you have heartened and helped—some easily named, some nameless.

The practices in this book are carefully constructed and graduated to increase your powers as an assisting force to more and more of those who need you—that is, of course, everyone.

Since our companions are not always tangible but are sometimes invisible, we might trust that many angels, saints, and bodhisattvas hover over us now, drawn into our heart arc by the magnetic power of our enthusiasm for this subject.

I even dare to hope that this book can become an assisting force for all of us:

Something,
We know not what,
is always and everywhere
lovingly at work,
we know not how,
to make the world more than it is now
to make us more than we are yet.
That Something is the assisting force:
a Higher Power than ego,
the impelling life force of evolution,

the inexhaustible lively energy of the universe,
our own enlightened nature.
All are one single reality,
a sacred heart of love, our heart at its best.

1 OUR ASSISTING FORCES

To accompany someone is to go somewhere with him or her, to break bread together, to be present on a journey with a beginning and an end. At a commencement like this, we're not sure exactly where the beginning might be, and we're almost never sure about the end. There's an element of mystery, of openness, in accompaniment: I'll go with you and support you on your journey wherever it leads. I'll keep you company and share your fate for a while. And by "a while," I don't mean a little while. Accompaniment is much more often about sticking with a task until it's deemed completed by the person or people being accompanied, rather than by the *accompagnateur*.

—Paul Farmer, "Accompaniment as Policy"

Some assisting forces are with us all our lives; others are with us temporarily. Some will step in to help us, for instance, when we find ourselves lost in a crisis or trauma. The Good Samaritan is an example of such a temporary assisting force. He saved the life of the victim of injustice by his compassion and generosity but, as far as the story goes, did not become a lifelong ally.

It can also seem to us that some of our allies were with us only temporarily when actually their energy is still animating us. The contribution of Martin Luther King Jr. to our society is an example in the socio-political realm. In the personal realm we may recall a high school teacher who helped us find our passion and aptitude for science or art, or maybe we had a coach or friend who saw talent in us when we did not. They are no longer tangibly present in our lives. Yet, if we have followed up on their encouragement and advanced in science, art, or any talent, they are, in an interior way, still with us, still cheering us on. Neither time nor distance make a difference in how the archetype of the assisting force stays with us.

The word "ally" is neutral, so it can refer to support and assistance either for positive or negative purposes. An ally in a crime is referred to as an accomplice or accessory. The ally in that instance collaborates with us in actions that cause harm. Such an ally connives with us in disregarding the social contract, thereby enlisting our negative, shadow side. But in this book, the word "ally" refers to the positive assisting presence. This type of ally is the helper on our journey to integrity, love, and wisdom—three ways we manifest our wholeness and live out our spiritual potential.

Our longing for an ally is inborn. Perhaps the experience of loneliness is the psyche's clever way of getting us to seek an alliance. This may explain why a lonely child makes up an imaginary friend. It may even help us understand why there are folk characters like Santa Claus who represent assistance, magically giving us what we want or need. Indeed, getting through the winter without some merry assisting presence is not an appealing option!

In religious traditions we notice beliefs about allies; guardian angels come to mind. Religious beliefs are reflections of the world of the higher Self. The deep psyche is holotropic—that is, it is characterized by an inner inexorable inclination in us to move in the direction of wholeness, the way a bud keeps directing itself to the sun for its full flowering. For us and for flowers too, growth is impossible if we remain isolated. The central religious promise is a response to this—a divine presence abides always and everywhere with us. In Buddhism a bodhisattva represents the same kind of presence. As we shall see in this book, in Buddhism the bodhisattvas are enlightened beings who love humanity so much that they choose not to partake of nirvana, freedom from rebirth, until they have helped all of us find enlightenment too. In other words, like the traditional God in a religion, and like all assisting forces, they are "always with us" especially in dark valleys.

We break through duality when we realize that spiritual and religious assisting forces reflect our own inner powers. Spiritual allies are ultimately interior. What we feel to be divine accompaniment is a contact with our own energies and potentials—personified as bodhisattvas, angels, saints, spiritual beings—helping us toward enlightenment. They reflect the full spectrum of spiritual powers in all of us. To see Buddha as our ally is actually our way of acknowledging enlightenment in ourselves: "The bodhisattvas are not glorified, exotic, unnatural beings, but simply our own best qualities in full flower," explains the Buddhist teacher Dan Leighton, in his book *Faces of Compassion*. In his Sermon 52, the German theologian Meister Eckhart described the same concept: "In a breakthrough, I find that God and I are both the same . . . sheer, pure, limpid unity, free of all duality." And Carl Jung concluded, "The world of gods and spirits is truly 'nothing but' the collective unconscious inside me."

"Allies" and "we" are nouns with overlapping meanings. "Assisting" is one verb describing what it takes to gain full participation in the web of life's family of allies. These allies amplify our identity and give us a name too grand to fit on any license. The assisting forces in our lives are part of the composition of our sense of self: "I am a part of all I have met," Aeneas jubilantly proclaimed in Virgil's epic. Throughout this book we will speak of ourselves and our assisting forces in separate terms, but we always keep in mind they are ultimately one and the same. We will see more about this as we go along.

Along these lines, we can remind ourselves to beware of magical thinking—superstition or irrational beliefs—about allies. Here are two examples:

- "Nothing bad can happen to me as long as *they* are in my life. I can trust I will be safe." This belief, actually a superstition, is contrary to the developmental task we all face: to take care of ourselves while we also ask for supplemental help—help that may or may not come to us as we expect.
- "If I am pitiable enough, a rescuer will come." We might even keep ourselves victims *so that* a rescuer will come. In healthy living, we go to an ally for support in building our own resources, not to grab on to the shirttails of a do-it-all-for-me savior. Allies are not rescuers; they are fellow heroes. Our best allies are the ones who show us how to be self-allies.

WHAT IS AN ARCHETYPE?

Jung theorized that an archetype is a component of our collective unconscious, an innate energy, a natural inclination in every human, like an instinct in an animal. Something indelibly within us clamors to live out a variety of energies. Examples of archetypes are mother, father, king, queen, hero, god, angel, saint, teacher, shadow, villain, demon, trickster, assisting and afflicting forces. The assisting force is an archetype in the unconscious of all of us, waiting to meet the one who offers it to us, ready to be the one who shows it to ourselves and others.

The archetypes are so-called because they are the same across all of humanity. Each is shown in an individual way. It will be up to each of us to act out one or more or all of these potentials of our mutual humanness. Since so many powers are intrinsic to our full emergence as humans, we fulfill ourselves when we live out their most positive energies. As an example, the archetype of a mother reflects an inherent motherliness in all of us, irrespective of gender. Only some people show this motherliness but all of us contain it. To show it even for a moment in a relationship can be how it is activated and will contribute to our wholeness. By "wholeness" we mean that our potentials are being actualized. And we have a "calling to wholeness," in which one or some of our potentials will be the contribution we make to the world. They will be the contributions that fit our natural talents and are a source of personal bliss. Talents we were born with give us a head start. Showing or practicing their energy to fulfill ourselves and help others is what is meant by a "calling."

An archetype can also be an energy that is affecting our experiences, attitudes, and behaviors. It can even become an organizing principle of our life choices and of our identity. For instance, perhaps we are helpers and our life is centered on that archetypal energy. It has become part of the design of our personality. An archetypal energy is then a hidden driving force or motivation behind our decisions. Any archetype becomes accessible when we become conscious of its presence and welcome its activation.

Archetypal energy is personified as a common character or motif in stories the world over. The reason we so easily recognize various archetypal characters in stories is precisely because they are already within us instinctively. Indeed, the full cast of archetypes has always resided in human nature. The stories and films we most remember are precisely the ones that present archetypal characters, themes, and events—for example, *The Wizard of Oz, Star Wars, The Matrix.*

An assisting force is also part of a larger archetype—the archetype of grace, the gift dimension of life. Graces are benefits that come to us without our having to merit or earn them. They help us traverse our path by opening us to wisdom and powers we thought were beyond us. Grace is not something extra dolloped onto us. It is part of the evolutionary drive that supports existence so life can keep moving beyond where it is, keep transcending its limits. This is the assisting force that advances all evolutionary growth. Allies anchor us and set sail with us on the human voyage beyond our truncated horizons. This is how allies are graces. Everything we can say about grace we can say about the assisting forces in and around us.

Some archetypes are personified—for example, God, saints, devils. Other archetypes are not characters but *events*—for example, dying and rising. In religion these mysterious events are made into rituals so we can participate in them—for example, baptism. Some of the events are about inner transformations—for example, epiphany, conversion, ascension. Literature and film have preserved archetypes in words and images and religion has preserved archetypes in beliefs, rituals, and images too. Archetypes also appear in dreams, what Freud called "the royal road to the unconscious." Dreams conduct us on that road.

We can best understand assisting forces as nondual, as ultimately interior forces. Some are external indeed—for example, helpful friends from our past. But the energy of assisting forces, their archetypal presence, is always in us. They are not "out there" but in here, in our human nature. Some are spiritual and invisible. Yet, they were already and always in our higher Self, who we are beyond ego. Our biggest challenge of faith is to believe who we are. An archetype can be a metaphor enacted in daily life through the roles and actions of people around us. When we say "it takes a village to raise a child," we mean that fathering and mothering are most helpful for our development when they come from a variety of sources. All the villagers will in various times and ways act as parents do: as nurturers, teachers, friends, encouragers, and helpers. There is a unique energy in each of the villagers, shown in unique ways but recognizable as the same parenting energy. The friendly man next door may be fulfilling a fathering archetype when he protects us, and his trickster humor may get us to laugh. Similar archetypes might also be recognizable in art: Mona Lisa's face seems to show a motherly character as well as that of a kindly friend.

Archetypes often appear in the roles of characters in stories. We read about them or see them on stage or screen and we relate to them personally. The *Star Wars* space rebel Han Solo is not a real-life ally, but we respond strongly to the energy, the archetype, of the assisting force in him. When we notice ourselves being responsive to certain characters in a play or film, we are seeing an archetype that is meaningful to us. In other words, we are recognizing ourselves or people we know. In their actions we might see what we are needing or avoiding.

We also notice that each character has a positive and negative side. In a story we may encounter the kindly mother or the witch mother, the assisting force as well as the afflicting force. Every archetypal energy is a coin with two sides. So are all the qualities in the human psyche, both light and dark.

In stories, universally, we see the same characters—hero, villain, assisting forces, trickster, mother, father, king, queen—all showing energies that are familiar. They are familiar not only because we see them over and over but because we have all the same energies in ourselves. Each of us is a village, a family, a cast of characters. That is the nature of being human, captured in the phrase *e pluribus unum*. "From many comes one" is not only a description of the United States; it is also a description of each of us as individuals: we are a variety of energies acting and interacting as one.

Archetypes can appear among groups—for instance, at work. Everyone in the office knows to whom to turn when it is time to see the humorous side of a difficult predicament. Everyone knows who has a listening ear, and who does not. And, of course, we are archetypes to others at home and work. Likewise, just as we might have looked to our older sister for mothering, people might see a family archetype in us. They then may rely on us to be that for them—important for us to notice, but up to us as to how we will respond. It is essential, especially in intimate relationships, to ask one another which energies each partner represents, which energies each may be relying on the other to show.

Finally, exactly the same archetypes frequently appear in traditional theistic terms. There is a father God, a divine Mother, saints who help us, demons who attempt to destroy us. To say we are "made in the image of God" clearly then implies that the various characteristics of the divine are those of humans too. Then, if we see with a faith perspective, our calling becomes exhibiting the positive divine qualities in our daily life. Faith will also mean trust that we are receiving continuous graces to do this. To see human nature as mirroring the divine shows us the infinite extent of our humanity. To see divine nature reflecting our own nature shows we believe that the Infinite is in love with finite us.

WE ALWAYS KNEW

It seems that belief in assisting forces has always been part of human experience. Think about the many things we do and ways we feel that attest to the widespread belief in the presence of assisting forces that give us an assurance that we are not alone:

- Longing for a relationship with the belief that it will end our loneliness (implying a need for an intimate other)
- Cherishing and feeling elated when we find kindred souls (implying we are only fully ourselves in the world of others)
- Taking a stand alone against a power stronger than ourselves (implying that we can gain help even from invisible assisting forces)
- Cooperation (implying there can be help from other people)
- Trusting people we don't know (implying that everyone has the assisting force energy within)
- Asking for help from a stranger (implying that it is reliably in human nature to be of help)
- Asking for feedback and advice from those we trust before we make big decisions (implying a need for insight from others)
- Finding comfort in knowing that we are not alone in our experience, problem, or illness but that others have it too (implying we are not isolated or unusual)

- Feeling comfy-cozy in a café though we don't know anyone, yet we feel we are surrounded by like-minded people as we sip coffee or work on our laptop
- Cherishing memories of those who loved us in childhood or later and feeling soothed
- Interior talking to those who loved us in life and have died
- Keeping objects that belonged to deceased loved ones as tokens of comfort
- Displaying photos of family members in our home and office, as if they were thereby actually with us
- Carrying a memento, photo, or religious object that represents a lasting presence or kinship connection
- Preserving family traditions
- Honoring anniversaries
- Praying with the belief that Someone is hearing us
- Turning to the three refuges in Buddhism: the Buddha, the Dharma, and the Sangha—that is, fellow practitioners
- Seeking connection with someone we love or whose company gives us pleasure because such connection provides an oxytocin-rich experience
- Staying in touch with friends
- Having and caring for a pet that accompanies us often or always
- Keeping a list of contacts on our desk or on our phone—and carrying it with us in case we need connection or assistance
- Having a go-to person whom we contact when we need comfort or perhaps a challenge
- Feeling safety and security when we are part of a group, including cliques or in-groups
- Bringing a friend or relative to be our advocate when we go into the hospital or to a doctor for something serious or scary
- Our eyes lighting up when we see a friend walk into our hospital room

- Being in and trusting the effectiveness of therapy
- Contributing to a charity that helps people we will never see or acting as a Good Samaritan toward someone in trouble
- Visiting the graves of loved ones and saying something to them
- Holding hands
- Walking someone home

In addition to these personal examples, here are some indicators that institutions in society work as assisting forces:

- Nations that form coalitions and alliances
- Parties that work in caucuses
- Elected and appointed officials who support democratic institutions and human rights, especially those of minorities
- Religions that support human rights and nonviolence
- Services associated with the upkeep of the infrastructure
- Emergency services such as firefighting, law enforcement, and medical and psychiatric programs
- Helping professions such as social work, counseling, and public health advocacy
- Service industries
- Suicide hotlines
- Disaster services
- Nonprofit agencies
- Charities and welfare
- Twelve-step programs
- Adoption services
- 9-1-1 dispatching

In Canada an "assisting force" is a technical term for help from one jurisdiction to another in an emergency, and the province minister is required to ask for the help. (Yet, as we shall explore later, archetypal assisting forces may find us even if we don't ask.)

An assisting force, whether visible or invisible, is an ally in several ways:

- Provides advocacy, mentoring, refuge, direction, nurturance, encouragement, accompaniment, companionship, sense of belonging and inclusion
- Reduces fear, isolation, despair
- Stays with us, stands up for us permanently or as long as needed
- Is a responsive resource in times of confusion, breakdown, or struggle, or steps in to protect or guide us when we are so stressed or traumatized that cortisol is making it impossible for us to think straight
- Shows us how to be self-assisting, rather than fostering dependency
- Does not ask for reciprocation but is open to it

WHEN WE LET IN OR PUSH AWAY OUR HELPERS

We can now explore the ways we let in or keep out assisting-force energy. We can look into ourselves—our behaviors, our choices—to see how we may be opening the door or slamming it shut in the face of a helper. We keep out assisting energy when our ego gets too big for us to hear it knocking for entry. The assisting force simply wants to help us open the potential that is in us, but we may sometimes choose instead to keep ourselves limited.

Letting In

One way to draw allies to us is to obey the *timing* that points us to going or staying—remaining under the breast or flying out of nest. When we go with whatever is ready to happen, the happening seems to have a *will* element in it, a mobilizing drive. We can align ourselves to that "move ahead" will. For instance, when we were adolescents we were ready to be more independent. Our minds and bodies were going in that direction—that is, moving us with what felt like will, a force driving us. It was up to us to join in—or rather dive into what was new—but in a way that was responsible too, as our parents and teachers were advising us.

This "both. . . and" style takes what in Buddhism is called "beginner's mind." We have to keep becoming novices, apprentices to the great task that faces all of us, to recognize our readiness to move ahead as individuals while yet maintaining interconnectedness—as in the example of adolescent development. It happens optimally in an environment of combining freedom with wise limit-setting.

At any time, we can remind ourselves that our helpers, human and otherwise, form an assisting circle around us. We can ask for their help: "All you bodhisattvas come to my aid." In the *Bhagavad Gita* (chapter 6, verse 30) we hear the divine welcome: "For those who see me everywhere and see all things in me, I am never lost, nor are they ever lost to me."

Another way to let in assisting forces is to become bold and not hold back on how much we dare request of them. We ask all and for all. Such daring takes letting go of dualism, since our spiritual allies are ultimately within us. Our boldness is then a path to finding our own divinity, everywhere and in us. Johann Wolfgang von Goethe stated it well: "Be bold and mighty forces will come to your aid." This is not magical thinking; it is something we humans have always noticed, and for which we can be thankful. Gratitude encourages assisting forces to join us.

Obi-Wan Kenobi encourages Luke Skywalker to "call upon the Force." That Force is not only the miraculous lightsaber but Luke's own inner power as well as a higher power. All three are one assisting force, visible and invisible. The "calling upon" is an invocation—traditionally called "prayer"; it is a request to a higher power for help. A believer's prayer for others can thus be an assisting force: For instance, as emeritus Pope Benedict XVI was dying, Pope Francis asked for prayers "to accompany him . . . on his pilgrimage." Pope Francis equated praying for someone with accompanying him, a quality of an assisting force. Ordinations in Catholic ritual begin with a choir singing the "Litany of the Saints." The choir sings out the name of a saint and the congregation sings back: "Pray for us." This call and refrain is an example of calling in, gathering the allies to bless the moment. Allies seem glad to assemble for us when we are open to them and invite them. It is not begging or demanding; it is invoking.

PRACTICE

CREATING A LITANY FOR CHALLENGING TIMES

Following the lead of the "Litany of the Saints," we might call upon all our own helpers and ancestors as we embark on a new phase of our own personal journey—whether that is a new career, a new relationship, or a new crisis. Try creating your own litany that invokes family and friends who feel to you like assisting forces. After each name use an invocation, such as "Be my guide, or support, or helper." Use the entire list in challenging times or when you embark on a new venture. Here are examples of what the litany looks like: "Granddad, be a guide to me," "Mike, help me through this," "Aunt Helen, stay by my side."

In his online "Daily Meditation" of February 12, 2023, the priest and writer Richard Rohr reflected, "I am increasingly convinced that the word 'prayer' . . . was meant to be a descriptor and an invitation to inner experience. When spiritual teachers invite us to 'pray,' they are in effect saying, 'Go inside and know for yourself!'" This interior experience is, of course, precisely what happens in contemplation, mindfulness meditation, or zazen. Chögyam Trungpa, in *The Tibetan Book of the Dead*, reminds us that, in the Buddhist tradition, "the word which is often translated simply as prayer means, literally 'wish-path' (Tibetan *smon-lam*). It is not a request to an external deity, but a method of purifying and directing the mind. It acts as inspiration by arousing *the mind's inherent desire for good, which attracts the fulfillment of its aim*" (my italics). The word "attracts" reflects the notion that we can indeed draw allies to ourselves so they can help us along and cheer us on—an idea invoked by the reluctant assassin to his fellow conspirator in Shakespeare's *Julius Caesar*: "Now bid me run, / And I will strive with things impossible; / Yea, get the better of them."

Pushing Away

How might we be pushing away those who want to support us— those we need for support? It is first of all the arrogant ego that may interfere with our building a support system: "I don't need anyone. I can go it alone." In a world of "inter-being" (to use the term coined by Thich Nhat Hanh) that rejection of support is a dangerous—and illusory—perspective. It is actually a disability, since no human has ever survived without help; help is a re-quirement for survival beginning at birth. When we say we won't depend on others in our old age, we are suffering from a truly life-threatening dysfunction. Or to use another example, a man who believes it is not manly to need anyone will suffer damaging problems with intimacy—when the only need he can admit having is the need for sex, true bonding can't happen.

Consider the various ways many of us sabotage our need for help, and the outcomes that result:

- We may feel unworthy of receiving help. We then stay stuck enacting the victim archetype: we don't reach for access or connection; we forfeit help by dismissing assisting forces. This refusal to open may not be rightly called "stuckness," then. It may be a decision.
- We may feel shame about seeking help. We may believe we are being weak when we ask for it. We lose an opportunity for

building the virtue of humility, essential if we are ever to admit our need for assisting forces.

- Growth is not only a process of addition. It is also about subtraction—it requires letting go of all the accretions smuggled into our psyches by unhealthy models of rugged individualism. To be freeze-framed in that ego stance vitiates our chances at the alliances that help us become all we can be.

- We may have a problem with trust, and consequently we may not trust the help that comes to meet us unbidden. But trust is a necessary requisite to any opening to an assisting force.

- We may distrust connection by assisting forces who come our way—including someone who wants a relationship with us—as a result of early or recent trauma. If connection, especially in childhood, has been too often followed by withdrawal or abuse, we may ever after be wary of those who want to bond with us. Our psyche has wrongly written the word "connection" with an arrow attached to it pointing to the words "danger of abandonment." The way to know this is happening is that we will feel bodily anxious before or after a *pleasant* time with someone. The fretful past is prejudicing the present. Our fear: "What happened before will happen again!" Being stuck in that paranoid fantasy holds us back from healthy bonding.

- In the context of an intimate relationship, a relationship of allies, we may feel we just can't get enough from the other. Then even too much is not enough. This "can't get enough" energy is yet another counterfeit safety measure against real closeness: "You can't fulfill me" is the same as "I don't need to be close to you or need you." When fear rules the roost, the assisting forces of love can't gain admittance.

- We may reject assisting forces when we say no to the summons to take the next step on our journey. Then, in a positive turn of events, we may be pulled into action by others, or by life events, or nature. In *The Wizard of Oz*, for example, we see Dorothy refusing to leave Kansas but a tornado tosses her into the Land of Oz, where wisdom awaits her. The tornado was nature's assisting force. For us it can work either way: we can say no and lose our opportunity, or we might be forced to say yes (as Dorothy was). Why not take a chance?

- Moving willingly from one era of life to another will invite assisting forces who help us engage in our transitions wisely and gracefully. Our willingness will mean that we have become able see the phases of life not as losses but as *progressions*. When, instead, we say no to what comes next we are also saying no to the assisting forces that await us at our next threshold.

TIME-OUT

We sometimes find ourselves in times of difficulties from which there seems to be no exit. In those moments, we can gain access to an assisting force with an attitude of yes to our predicament, no matter how gloomy it is. We put up no resistance to whatever life situation is facing us, no matter how far it is beyond our control, no matter how unpleasant or scary it has become. If we feel destabilized by distressing moments we can restabilize by surrendering to what we cannot change—a paradoxical healing. Our embrace of the affirmation about "the serenity to accept the things we cannot change" can open the door to the world stepping in to help us. Indeed, reality itself has its own brand of assisting forces that arise from within and around us if we patiently pause or willingly wait. The Jungian therapist Helen Luke has written that "the real goal of all our efforts is to arrive at the capacity for this goalless waiting." Trusting this archetypal fact about how the spiritual world works is the foundation of healthy optimism.

Surrender to reality can be fostered by a practice of contemplative sitting, a silent openness to reality without attachment to any object, finding an answer or craving a solution. The word "contemplation" in Latin refers to "staying in the boundaries of the temple"—in other words, stay put and the gift will come. We forget that sometimes we are not called upon to be active in the public forum. Sometimes we are meant simply to sit, like monks, poets, or Sitting Bull. Both styles have a legitimate place on the heroic journey. We see Robin Hood alone in prison, pondering his fate as he waits to be hanged. His silence is nonetheless followed by rescue. We see Pinocchio lying water-logged on the beach as a prelude to a visit from the Blue Fairy, the spiritual assisting force to his becoming a real boy. All heroes and heroines seem to require a time-out from their derring-do. This intentional rest is how they nourish and equip themselves for the next adventure.

At those times when we have to surrender to reality, we may feel that our journey has been *interrupted*. But when we gladly say yes to what is, we find out it was only our expectations that were intruded upon, not our actual life story. We come to realize that the "interruption" has actually presented us with a new set of options. When we assent graciously to life as it is we suddenly awaken to new paths. We engage in innovative ways of living that accommodate what we no longer view as an interruption—we now consider it an intermission.

We human mountaineers are geared for a climb but may sometimes forget that a time-out is part of the undertaking. We miss the point when we think the heroic journey requires only that we "keep moving." If we move into quiet time or contemplation, we might find it to be not a halt to the journey but an initiation into its next phase or a respite to rally new energies. This recovery time is yet another way to access inner allying resources. Our time-out can then be a way of gestating, of letting the dough silently rise after the kneading has been completed.

In a time-out the form of the helper may not be external. Our assisting force may be simply be a commitment to staying present in the dark night of the soul or in a lonely time in the desert. There we can find a new wisdom, a wisdom of trusting ourselves—settling into the power of just sitting, just being open to what may unfold. It seems that Marcel Proust knew this too:

"We do not receive wisdom, we must discover it for ourselves, after a journey through the wilderness which no one else can make for us and from which no one can spare us." In other words, in our aloneness we come to realize that we can be self-assisting.

Albert Camus wrote in an essay about his epiphany upon returning to a place from his youth: "In the midst of winter, I found there was, within me, an invincible summer." In a bleak winter landscape we know without doubt that there is a process of growth churning beneath the frozen ground. In the same way, we can trust that in our darkest, seemingly promiseless moments there is growth happening somewhere inside us and it will bud when the time is right.

The Jesuit priest Pedro Arrupe kept a journal—a memoir of the soul—while he was held in solitary confinement as a prisoner of war in Japan during World War II. In one impressive journal entry, he describes contacting an inner ally: "Alone as I was, I learned the knowledge of silence, of loneliness, of harsh and severe poverty; the interior conversation with the 'guest of the soul' who had never shown himself to be more sweet than then." This priest's experience reminds us that a heroic journey does not always mean traveling or battling. A legitimate episode of the journey involves floating buoyantly on the waves rather than gallantly riding them. We don't need to tread water valiantly either; we can trust the tides of life to take us where we need to go.

Too often we are like Ulysses, who believed he could only be his authentic self in the active phases of the hero archetype—in his case, that of a brazen warrior. As the aged "idle king" of Ithaca, he did not understand that the time had come for him to sit in meditation, ponder his legacy, perhaps write his memoirs, attend a philosophy school, write a new poem. "You only need sit still long enough in some attractive spot in the woods that all its inhabitants may exhibit themselves to you by turns," advises Henry David Thoreau in *Walden*. Sitting can lead to seeing.

2 THE FORCE WITHIN US

With few exceptions our members find that they have tapped an unsuspected inner resource which they presently identify with their own conception of a Power greater than themselves.

—*Alcoholics Anonymous*, "The Big Book"

Our first and main ally is our deepest identity beyond our limited personality—that is, the higher Self. In her poem "The Journey," Mary Oliver narrates the internal process of someone (addressed as "you") gaining a "new" voice that will serve as company on a quest to redeem her life—a process that includes slowly recognizing that the seemingly new voice is in fact "your own." The implication is that the first and ultimate assisting force is right here inside us—or rather we are right here inside a vast it. That "it" is not a noun; it is a verb meaning all that holds and nurtures us in the web of life, the omnipresence of the divine, our authentic identity, the "more than" the superficial details on our driver's license. Our biggest challenge is to believe we are more than ever we thought. My own most constricting addiction is clinging to the version of Dave this mind of Dave insists I am—and have to be. I often wonder, "Will I ever meet the Dave who is trying to emerge?"

What Carl Jung called the Self is ultimately a phoenix energy, our ever newly arising power. This higher-Self-than-ego *is* the unfailing interior ally, our true nature. Jung called the higher Self "the God within," since it has the qualities ordinarily associated with the divine: eternal, infinite, transcendent, healing. Our higher Self is inherently *more than* appearances do or can disclose. It also holds the wisdom of all humans from time immemorial. Thus we can rely on an oracular *inner* voice. When we nudge our ego aside and make contact with our true Self we have arrived at Delphi, residence of divine wisdom.

Our transcendent inner identity may also come through to us as an interior presence—it may be experienced as "company," as Mary Oliver writes in "The Journey." Abraham Lincoln expressed a similar idea in the course of arguing against the repeal of the Missouri Compromise in 1864: "I desire so to conduct the affairs of this administration that if, at the end, when I come to lay down the reins of power, I have lost every other friend on earth, I shall at least have one friend left, and that friend shall be down inside of me." He sees the higher Self as a friend, an ally keeping him company especially in toughest times. The assisting-force archetype is not outside but in us, not beside us but inside us.

For some, our higher Self as inner ally is a spiritual resource that comes through for us in times when we are caught in inner conflict such as addiction. Whatever it is we become addicted to seems, at first, to be an assisting force because it helps us escape from an unappealing reality. Soon enough, though, we recognize it as an afflicting force damaging our lives and relationships. Then we may open to the grace that shows us our need for recovery. Wonderfully, the afflicting force of addiction folds and the assisting force of healing unfolds.

OUR BODYMIND AND EGO

"My mind to me a kingdom is . . ." declared the Renaissance poet Edward Dyer, adding that whatever he lacks, his mind provides. In seeming contrast, the transcendentalist poet Walt Whitman proclaimed "I sing the body electric." But these lyric celebrations of creative mind and dynamic physicality are not contradictory—the mind is not limited to the brain. There is mind in our bodies too, and both our mind and body are assisting forces in all of us. To put it another way, our psyche comprises more than our higher Self. It also includes what we call "mind," mediated through neuronal activity in the brain. Our minds contain faculties—that is, innate capacities. They become useful abilities, assisting forces, when we invest them in the best interests of our development and the fulfillment of our life goals. Examples of faculties are thought, memory, imagination, will, instinct, sensation, emotion. To this list we can add conscience, which is both innate and acquired.

The "ego," in Jung's view, is our conscious mind. It is sometimes an assisting force, sometimes an afflicting force. When it helps us make wise assessments and act on them it is wholesome and helpful, an assisting force. Then our ego is the ally that helps us achieve our goals in life.

When our ego is inflated (too big) or deflated (too small), it becomes an afflicting force—it gets in the way of goal fulfillment. What we call the "big ego" is a mindset, not a property of the brain. When our ego is inflated we might find it hard to collaborate with others and respect their contributions to a project, for example. An inflated ego gets in the way of our fulfilling two healthy human goals: relating and participating in productive interactions with others.

An ego that is deflated, on the other hand, impoverishes our self-esteem. We find it hard to trust ourselves or to believe we have any valuable contribution to make to the world around us. We might see ourselves as victims or as people with no inner resources. We feel we are "less than" rather than equal to others.

A healthy ego is characterized by an emotionally secure or strong sense of oneself. A healthy ego serves as a part of our own mind that "keeps us company" in the form of thoughts, ideas, solutions, creative imagination, and authentic feelings. This is a way for ego to be ally.

Feelings themselves become allies when we hold them in balance rather than exaggerate their importance or amplify our way of expressing them. We are not meant to be possessed by feelings and subjugated to them. On the other hand, when we diminish the importance of our feelings or inhibit their expression, we are subjugated by fear, the ego's way of coopting our self-esteem. Either way we lose valuable allies. Feelings actually gain us allies. Perhaps our tears are visible so others can see them and feel compassion and comfort us—just what truly assisting forces do.

Activating our healthy ego as an inner ally happens through our commitment to doing our psychological work and engaging in our spiritual practices. An adult doing inner-child work is an ally of the healthy maturation of the child self. People committed to a program of recovery from drug addiction are enlisting the assisting force of a spiritual program that restores them to sanity.

Sometimes working on ourselves can mean openly looking at what we're up to. Sometimes our bodymind ally protects us from directly looking at a traumatic event by engaging in dissociation: we find an exit, a mental distraction from the full impact of trauma around and in us. This inner ally protects us from fully knowing or even naming whatever is happening until we are ready to hold the information safely. Often this cannot happen until adulthood, and in the context of therapy. In fact, trying to know our own truth before we are ready for it blocks the discovery of it. A trauma comes with built-in time clock. It will not chime its name until we are ready to know it. This is how early trauma *protects* us. Yet throughout our lives the body tells its tale anyway. Our body is the spokesperson of our psyche's predicament. In that sense, the body is the assisting force manifesting as a whistleblower. The psychological part of us protects us from knowing more than we can handle. The somatic part of us shows us our truth but seldom in a way that is explicit. Close attention to our bodies and feelings shows us where the ancient bruises are. And every bruise is a door to self-knowledge.

THE USEFULNESS OF DAILY
STRESSES AND LIMITATIONS

Negative experiences as well as disturbing thoughts or feelings can be assisting forces. For instance, we may feel regret about how we have hurt others or let ourselves be hurt. We may feel remorse for the many mistakes we have made in life. It is normal for any of us sometimes to be plagued with regrets about past choices. Under each regret lies our own shame about how inadequate or wrong we believe we so often have been. Memories rise from untidy graves to haunt us. It is as if our body knows we are inching closer to death every passing day and it wants to clear up any unresolved griefs before we depart. We can allow this bodily process by feeling our grief rather than running from it or staying stuck in regret: *when we run from our feelings we become a secret kept from ourselves and we forfeit knowing who we are.*

In a 1989 essay titled "When the Teacher Fails," the Buddhist practitioner Stephen T. Butterfield writes about the energizing self-discovery that resulted when he deliberately examined his faults:

> Empowered to turn negativity into a resource, I found flowering in me an unconditional cheerfulness and patience that is indestructible, because it is not based on the rejection of obstacles. I learned truly effective methods of confronting my arrogance, stinginess, jealousy, anger, and dullness, my ego-based patterns of behavior and belief. I learned how to crack these habits open and discover the luminous, enlightened energy frozen within them—energy which became available for creative work and joy. . . . I developed immense respect for my mistakes; without them, my discoveries could not have been made.

Regret about any experience can be a gateway rather than an obstruction. We can look back at our regrets and look forward to choices that transcend or reverse them. We can mourn and let go after a loss and the loss becomes a dharma gate—an opening, an ally conducting us into a new spiritual awareness and consequent maturation. To let go is to let flow. This letting go is how regrets or any distresses can turn into assisting forces.

PRACTICE
CULTIVATING THE INTERNAL GURU

Chögyam Trungpa Rinpoche remarks about the "internal guru" that "when the internal guru begins to function, then you can never escape the demand to open." To cultivate this opening, keep the following intentions in mind:

- We let go of craving and clinging, both "causes of suffering" as the Buddha describes them. In this regard, we keep in mind that having preferences is not a cause of suffering. Indeed, we need them to help us make wise choices. (Preferences lead us to eat raspberries but not poison berries. It is clinging to our preferences compulsively or forcing them on others that causes suffering.)
- We do not demand too much attention or assistance from anyone in our support system. Our healthy style is to turn to our allies but not to cling to them.
- We accept the fact of impermanence, one of the foundations of Buddhist teaching and a useful practice for saying yes to what is, as it is—a practice of gratitude captured in Shakespeare's immortal lines of farewell: "Let us be thankful / For that which is."

Opening in these ways can feel threatening. We all know that our limited range of vision and hearing doesn't let in the full extent of distracting sights and sounds around us. Yet our limited range is not a disability. It keeps us from overincorporating environmental stimuli. Thus the limits we set on what we let in has survival value. This habit of ours hearkens back to ancient times. Without careful choice about what to focus on, our ancestors might not have noticed the gold of the approaching saber-tooth tiger because they were so entranced by the streaks of golden sunlight in the nearby trees.

When fear is the issue that possesses us we will need someone to encourage us—that is, staying with us in our fear but cheering us on too. Sometimes we may even need our whole support system, visible and invisible, in order to restabilize ourselves. We call on those around us and beyond us to help us get back on track. We accept the given of life that everyone is at a loss at times: *shame about our own limits becomes humility when we realize we are just like other people.*

It is surely a given that we are all limited. It follows then that we all need to ask for help. Our symptoms and inner bankruptcies can then also be visits from the ally of wisdom. Anxiety and depression are allies when they point us to what is stressing or limiting us and may then serve to awaken our innate healing powers. In the symptom is a remedy: *We have all that it takes to awaken right now no matter how messed up we think we are.*

When everything turns out wrong, can we see it as a signpost that directs us to a new possibility, as in this poem by the Japanese samurai poet Mizuta Masahide?

My barn
Having burned down,
I now can see the moon.

BEING AN ALLY TO OURSELVES

Write this out in your own words or use mine. Say it aloud for three days in the morning and again at bedtime*:* "I look at my story as a mindful witness, not as a victim. Then I notice I hold my mistakes and inadequacies with compassion rather than judgment. I can even greet the future with curious excitement rather than fear. I have become my own trusted companion."

On the final day, spontaneously write a poem showing what has happened in you as a result of your affirmation. The next day or days, work on emending your poem so that it improves in quality and imaginativeness.

Working assiduously on the poetics of a poem simultaneously expedites our work on the issue it is about. There is a direct link between making a better poem and advancing the work we are doing on ourselves psychologically.

I wonder if Emily Dickinson did this same thing in her writing. After all, her poems were mostly journal entries about her feelings and experiences. Yet she carefully worked on them until they became highly skillful and unusually inventive. Caring about what we create, wanting it to be the best it can be, is parallel to how we work on our own growth.

IN OUR DREAMS

Images and actions in dreams, especially recurring dreams, are powerful assisting forces on our journey: "Dreams *prepare, announce, or warn* about situations long before they happen," wrote Carl Jung. When we are attentive to dreams, they perform the same healing service to our psyche as does a shrine of a saint or of a Buddha. We are looking into our own ever-translucent true nature. But dreams don't easily yield these gifts, don't clearly tell their tale. For this to happen, we have to engage in dreamwork, ponder and open the dream—preferably the very next day. Let's begin our path to this possibility by looking at dreams and then engage in a useful practice to work with them. This deliberate process is how dreams become skillful means of enlightenment.

The maker of dreams is the higher Self, in its role as the assisting force who escorts us into our deep psyche—that is, the unconscious. In a dream, the dream maker is addressing the ego about what it needs to know, what it does not know yet. Dreams show us what we may be hiding from ourselves and are now ready to know. For instance they might show us what has become one-sided in our attitudes, what we don't have enough of, what we have too much of, where we are caught in perplexing dilemmas.

Some dreams attempt to compensate, make up for a one-sidedness in our conscious life. For instance, a dream in which we are extremely passive may be telling us we need more get-up-and-go in our daily life. The reverse can also be true. A dream can depict us as aggressive when we need to be gentler. The dream maker uses the events, characters, and events of the day as props. Thus we don't discount the meaningfulness of a dream image just because it reminds us of what happened recently by saying, "I only dreamed of an oriole because I saw one yesterday." This minimization undermines a possible symbolic meaning ready to be mined.

Dreams also serve as signposts and mileposts on the journey from encapsulation in ego concerns to fearless engagement with the higher Self. This process is meant to help us forge what Jung calls an "ego-Self axis." In that axis, our conscious ego choices match the qualities of the higher Self: unconditional love, ageless wisdom, and the healing of divisions. Dreams help us see how effectively we are loving, how much wisdom we are activating, how much healing is still waiting to happen. Dreams give us hints about what new steps we can take to cultivate those three luminous life dedications. In this sense, dreams help us change, grow, move ahead, open up—all the gifts an assisting force so generously gives us.

Since dreams link conscious and unconscious they happen not in the intellect but at a "soul" level—another word for the kinship between them. Dreams are mostly made up of images. In fact, the soul is made up of a library of images. These images exist in two categories. Some are personal, from our family album. Some are beyond us as individuals—that is, they are transpersonal, hearkening from the wisdom scriptures of all ages and nations. This distinction reflects Jung's ideas about the unconscious as both personal and collective.

The dreams that are personal in content and meaning show us blind spots in our daily life and they point us to our personal goals. In those dreams, the characters usually appear as picture-perfect. Collective—that is, transpersonal—archetypal dreams use universal symbols and the characters are usually strangers to us though they may remind us of people we know. These dreams have a much stronger impact on us. They are also easier to remember. They tell a story that is like a myth, with characters and events that are more than ordinary—as in, spiritually alive.

Dreaming is part of everyone's sleep cycles. We usually dream every hour and a half or so. Unfortunately our dreams find their way into our short-term memory, so we might have trouble recalling them. The dream maker wants us to remember but asks that we do our part so it can happen. Jung says, "Attention to the unconscious pays it a compliment that guarantees its cooperation." To take advantage of the value of dreams, try the following approaches for remembering them:

- Be willing to remember, willing to do what it takes to remember, affirm to yourself that you are remembering your dreams.
- Wake up naturally rather than using an alarm clock (which may interrupt a dream).

- Keep a pad and pen by your bed and write down your dream as soon as you awaken. You do not have to write in paragraph form, only in phrases. Later, when you are out of bed and look at what you wrote, you will access more details automatically.
- When you get out of bed or reach for a way to record your dream, avoid sharp quick movements—they trip the short-term memory and you will then be less likely to remember your dream.
- Tell your dream to someone. This person does not have to be a therapist. In addition, tell the dream to yourself, silently in your mind. Hearing a dream externally and internally helps anchor it in consciousness.
- When you tell the dream always begin with the setting: for example, "I am back in high school." Be sure to put the whole dream into the present tense when you tell it. This language of immediacy makes it more real. Retell the dream at least once, and notice what new details you have added or remembered.
- Record your now-more-detailed dream in a dedicated dream journal.
- Notice if your most recent dream is totally new or like other dreams you have had—notice if it is a repetition of a former dream or a repetition of a former theme. Recurrent dreams are more apt to be pointing you to something that has been clamoring for attention and is ready to be examined and resolved.
- No one can interpret a dream fully, so don't try. Simply let it reside in you and wait for each character in the dream to help you understand what the message or insight might be.
- As mentioned above, dreams may compensate for whatever is exaggerated, partial, or missing in daily life. In addition, dreams may forecast a change, help us work through part of a trauma, show us where our work is, warn us of a danger. Ask your higher Self, the dream maker, which of these options might fit your dream. To accomplish all this, Jung suggests using a technique he called "active imagination." This practice

simply means working with the dream images and characters so they reveal what they are about in your life. Jung called it "dreaming the dream onwards."

ACTIVE IMAGINATION

A dream is a summary, an outline in symbol and metaphor; active imagination opens it up and clarifies the significance behind the symbols and metaphors. The active imagination technique is best accomplished by writing in your dream journal:

1. Begin with a minute or two of self-calming in silence.
2. Open to whatever you feel wants to come through from this experience. Affirm that you trust that dreams and active imagination are assisting forces in finding out about yourself in a profound way.
3. Have a conversation with each character in the dream; each can then become an ally of your own awakening consciousness. Remind yourself of exactly what you felt during the dream and what you felt when you woke up. Include what you feel bodily in the moment and in the dream.
4. Take the part of each character or thing and tell the dream from that point of view.
5. Ask: How is what happened in the dream like what is happening in my life right now or challenging me to change what I am doing? What are the characters in the dream saying to me?
6. Look at the dream image that most powerfully struck you. Examine your "felt sense" of it—that is, how and where you feel it bodily.
7. Look at what you have written and choose nine words that strike you. Make them into a short poem.

8. Turn something in the dream into a drawing, or sculpture, or a body movement.

9. Emma Jung wrote, in *The Holy Grail*, "There is an inner wholeness that presses its still unfulfilled claims upon us." Ponder her words, then reply to the following two questions in your dream journal: What claim does this dream make on me? How is this dream inviting me to make up for something that is missing or overdone in my life experience, relationships, actions, or feelings?

10. Turn what you see as the main point of the dream and your work on it into an affirmation you use throughout the day.

11. Show thanks to the dream maker by enacting a short ritual that brings closure to this practice and includes gratitude for all you are learning. Acknowledge dreams as assisting forces that help you. In this context, it is the daily practice of gratitude that makes us *aware* of our assisting forces. In that practice, our gratitude helps us do what dreams do: complete something. Surely this is why we say "thank you" *after* we receive a gift!

In working with images and figures in dreams we keep in mind the importance of moving back and forth between the objective meaning and our subjective take on it. For instance, you dream of an altar. Objectively, an altar is found at a religious site and is used for sacrifice. Subjectively, you may have a home altar for honoring saints, bodhisattvas, or cherished ancestors. Your work on the personal and transpersonal meanings of the altar in your dream is richly revealing when you combine those two directions: moving from objective to subjective and back again. Thereby you may find a link that speaks volubly to your present life condition. Finding that link is how an image becomes an ally.

For instance, I had a dream in which I was with my grandchildren—Siena, age nine, Nate, age five, and I am holding infant Nick. In the dream, we are walking down a street when suddenly we come upon an open cardboard box containing lively kittens, only a few weeks old. They are intertwined playfully with one another. I am delighted and I pet the head of a gray one. I wonder if it is safe to have the grandchildren pet them, pondering whether the kittens might scratch their hands. Then my attention turns to the kittens and I realize I can't leave them in public where someone might harm them. I feel obliged to find them good homes.

When I awoke I realized all that happened in the dream was in keeping with what I believe is my personality style: I would indeed be careful for the safety of my grandchildren. I would be touched by the lost or orphaned. I would feel obliged and responsible for the weak or abandoned. And I might even keep the gray kitten or offer it to the kids.

I asked myself what I felt in each scene of the dream, after I awoke: "How is this true in your life right now?" or "How is this not happening enough?" When we also dialogue with the characters in our dream, we see sides of ourselves overlooked before. It helps to take the part of each character and tell the dream from that person's, or in this case, each of the children's and the kitten's point of view. This attention to each character is how each can become an ally, a spirit guide for longer than just one night.

Last night I dreamed I was working in an agency and was arranging for a meeting room at the request of my boss. When I woke up I suddenly realized that a long-standing theme in my dreams has been giving assistance to someone I admire or being of service to those who need me. This style reflects my calling over the years to be of help to others—for example, in the way I am a writer of self-help books such as this one. Perhaps a recurrent theme or image in our dreams gives us a clue to our central archetype in life. We can ask ourselves what role we have most often played in our dreams. The answer may reveal something about our life purpose and the graces, the assisting forces, that came along to help us fulfill it.

3 ALLIES EVERYWHERE

One by one . . . I call before me the whole vast anonymous army of living humanity; those who surround me and support me though I do not know them; those who come, and those who go . . . and who today will take up again their impassioned pursuit of the light.
—Pierre Teilhard de Chardin, *Hymn of the Universe*

We saw in the preceding chapter that our main allies are forces within us: our higher Self, our bodymind, our dreams, and even the symptoms and limitations we deal with daily. Now we visit the pageant of other allies in the world around us. Some are human; many more are not.

Perhaps we can indeed see allies everywhere. Today, when I woke up with this book on my mind I thought, in a droll but realistic way, that every material thing is somehow an assisting force helping us live our lives: a bed for sleeping, a stove for cooking, a floor to walk on, a computer for writing this book, a chair for you to read it in.

THE PEOPLE WHO HELPED US

In an address to Harvard Divinity School in 1938, the transcendentalist Ralph Waldo Emerson spoke of the importance of holding in memory "the few interviews we have had with souls that made our souls wiser, that spoke what we thought, that told us what we knew, that gave us leave to be what we only are." We can remember or remain aware of such "souls," or allies, in our own lives. Allies in the world around us appear in many forms and can be described by many terms:

Adjutant	Copilot	My other half
Adviser	Coworker	Ombudsman
Advocate	Custodian	Pal
Affiliate	Defender	Partisan
Aide	Elder	Partner
Assistant	Empathic witness	Patron
Associate	Exemplar	Promoter
Auxiliary	Fairy godmother	Prompter
Backer	Friend	Protector
Backup	Go-to	Right-hand man
Benefactor	Guardian	(or woman)
Buddy	Guide	Role model
Caregiver	Guiding spirit	Sentinel
Cheerleader	Guru	Shaman
Coach	Helping hand	Sidekick
Cohort	Helpmate	Soulmate
Collaborator	Intimate	Sponsor
Colleague	Kindred spirit	Supporter
Companion	Listening ear	Teacher
Comrade	Mate	Teammate
Confederate	Mediator	Tutelary spirit
Confidant	Mentor	Wingman

These are not simply characters we might happen to bump into along life's corridor. They are the cast of characters necessary for our human story to unfold effectively. As we have been seeing, we are hardwired as social beings—companions are essential to human experience. "Without the conscious acknowledgment of our fellowship with those around us, there can be no synthesis of personality," wrote Carl Jung. "Individuation"—that is, psychological and spiritual maturation—"does not shut out the world but gathers it to oneself. . . . You cannot individuate on Everest."

This comment on the importance of connection is actually more than saying we are social beings. Our development as humans *requires* the cooperation of those who support our growth. They are not only helping us; they have become builders of the structure of our identity. We are who we are today because of their contributions over the years. Our solidarity with those we have known and loved has contributed to who we are and how we are. Our identity is not locked in our own bodymind; it includes the influences of our assisting forces. Indeed, the word "influence" is based on Latin roots meaning "flowing into."

Our main and most reliable human allies are the people who love us. Conversely, we are the allies of those we love. Love can be most simply described as a "caring, committed connection." All three of those words indicate alliance—that is, solidarity. In other words, love can only happen in an atmosphere of committed companionship—exactly what an assisting force is all about.

As is the case with any ally, we don't have to be with someone every moment to feel loved and cared about. We can hold the memory of special moments of true intimacy and go back to them at any time. We can even summon them up in our image-rich bodyminds to stabilize ourselves when we feel desolate or alone.

Perhaps we have been gathering such interior companions all our lives and they are at our side whenever we need them. These allies are all the people who really love and loved us. They somehow remain with us without having to be physically present. The reverse is also true—our faces appear in the inner circle of love of those we have loved. At this very moment you or I might be helping someone find solace or courage—simply through their memory or thought of how we love them. Memory is one of the main ways assisting forces stay alive in us. What is real endures. Both in our loving bonding with others and in theirs toward us, we know love is real because it *abides*.

Every friend is an ally but not every ally is a friend. The Good Samaritan was friendly but not a personal friend of the wounded man he helped. The Samaritan was a stranger who become caringly connected and committed—the components of love, so ultimately a stranger no more. The memory of him as an assisting force would likely remain in the heart of the victim he so generously helped.

Allies are not always at the same level as we in the realm of need or resource:

- Some are *equal* to us in wisdom or maturation; they are at our same level, coexplorers with similar gear who nonetheless can be of help by supporting and joining us on the path.
- Some *exceed* us in skill, so we learn from them or follow their lead and we benefit by following the landmarks they construct— often they are older than we, as in the familiar character of the wise old man or woman.
- Some are *less* skilled than we, so we teach or lead them—a practice that helps us grow too; thereby they become assisting forces in our life, an example of gaining by giving.

The words "exceed" and "less" do not imply hierarchy. True accompaniment is a side-by-side experience, not top-down. It is more like solidarity than charity. Likewise, it is not only first aid but ongoing follow-up.

Let's look at each of these three levels in detail, starting with the allies who are *equal*. They are our fellow travelers, our peers. These might be our friends, colleagues, fellow workers, siblings— people who seem to be at our level or stage in life.

Next are the archetypal examples of allies *at a higher level* than we. These include the sage, the seer, the guru, the teacher, the exemplar, the wise old adviser. They are personifications of the archetype of wisdom and encouragement. At a more tangible level they are the authors, teachers, therapists, models, and mentors who have moved us, who have helped us find ourselves, who have deeply inspired us. "At times," said Albert Schweitzer, "our own light goes out and is rekindled by a spark from another person. Each of us has cause to think with deep gratitude of those who have lighted the flame within us." Healthy people honor those gracious allies who exceed them in knowledge, skill, or courage. The unhealthy response is envy, which only creates bitterness and a loss of the opportunity to learn and grow. When envy is replaced by admiration we have found the assisting force we can learn from.

Some allies who "lighted the flame" did so for an entire population. Reinhold Niebuhr, in writing the famous "Serenity Prayer" now familiar in twelve-step programs,* was actually receiving a wisdom-grace that would then become a grace to so many all over the world. There is an ally power in the universe that wants to help all of us. It produces helpful writers, teachers, heroes, and enlightened beings who proclaim their wisdom and assistance in just the right words or deeds. We are all beneficiaries of these allies of humanity. And each of us can make a contribution by doing for others what others do for us. After all, grace comes to us only to move through us.

We can also find allies in those who have *less skill* than we do. As we saw above, those we help bring out our wisdom and compassion. In this context we recall that, to a new generation, elders may seem inferior to confer with because they appear to be old-fashioned or too conservative in their ideas. Yet elders are frequently allies who give us advice or feedback that is helpful precisely because of their long experience. To find ways for young

---

* Niebuhr's original version, from 1943, reads, "God give us grace to accept with serenity the things that cannot be changed, courage to change the things that should be changed, and wisdom to know the difference." "The things" in this prayer can include our personality traits!

and old to talk to one another and hear one another is an excellent way to form alliances that help us all. The Quaker peace activist George Lakey observed one gathering in which younger members "remarked on the value of seeing older activists with real differences talk with each other as allies alert for the emergence of common ground."

A character moving *between higher and lower levels* is the familiar sidekick we met in the introduction to this book. Such characters appear most often in Westerns and adventure tales, and they are usually more extraverted and audacious than the brooding hero. Sidekick characters have the common touch. They are more sensible about limitations, including those of their admirable hero. The sidekick is not only willing to perform lowly tasks that seem below the lofty hero but also may even be the one who saves the hero—for instance, when the hero has become incapacitated. Sometimes the sidekick is an equal to the hero—both helping and learning from the lead character. (We see this in Dr. Watson's relationship to Sherlock Holmes.) Moreover (as with Sancho Panza in the Don Quixote story), a sidekick inevitably brings in the note of humor so necessary to a good story.

Sidekick assistance does not only move in one direction. The hero will at some point in the story help or rescue the sidekick. Their roles are ultimately interchangeable. In fact, the ally in any tale—including the tale of our own lifetimes—returns the favor of help to the helper. In the movie story, the three friends on the road to Oz help Dorothy, but she also helps each of them. In real life, many of us were nurtured by our mother and later in life we will find ourselves helping her. We will see throughout this book that our receiving help becomes a call to be of help.

In my childhood, comic books focused on heroes like Superman, who operated alone, or Batman who had one helper, Robin. I have noticed while reading to my grandchildren that in comics now there is almost always a group of "super friends" rather than single heroes with one sidekick. Some comics nowadays show how a calamity requires the collaboration of many rescuers—it takes the joint effort of Superman, Batman, Robin, Green Lantern, and others to restore order successfully. Perhaps the new generation of young people may value coalition over "just-me" heroism. They may have a sense of assisting forces as *collaborative*.

FELLOWSHIP

Fellowships are examples of alliances that lead to healing, enlightenment, and growth. The fellowship of practitioners in Buddhism helps each other toward enlightenment. The fellowship of members of twelve-step programs contribute to each other's recovery from addiction. Both fellowships recognize that we can't rely only on ourselves for healing or enlightenment—we need assistance. Indeed, the very first step toward any transformation is admitting that we are powerless without help.

As an aside, an admission about our condition as a step toward recovery applies also to acceptance of our emotional problems. A psychological paradox is that we are more likely to change when we accept ourselves in all our woundedness. Now we see why this is so: to accept ourselves as needing help is to invite healing and transformation from a higher power than our ego can conjure or construct. Paradoxically, our total yes to our neediness can lead us to a fulfillment of it. We can ask for this fulfillment or it can come to us on its own—sometimes with a wonderfully wide welcoming wink.

The Buddhist fellowship, the Sangha, is one of the three refuges on the path to enlightenment. A refuge is a "go to" when we are suffering, stressed, or in peril. We then turn to the Buddha, our own awakened mind-heart. We turn to the Dharma, the Buddhist teachings engraved on every mind, body, and heart. We turn to the

Sangha, our fellow practitioners. This Sangha does not have to be our own familiar, local group. It can be universal when we have a sense of kinship with any people in the world who suffer or seek as we do. We are always and everywhere one with all people who are moving toward awakening. Our practice of the Dharma is how we serve the universal Sangha. We do not sit on the meditation cushion alone; practitioners the world over are with us.

The word "with" keeps coming up in our discussion. Indeed, it is the key to all that alliance is about. We can endure any "what" as long as there is a "with." And, as our spiritual consciousness expands, the "with" is recognized as a "within." In that moment, duality, the cause of so much suffering and ignorance, disappears and we appear as we really are, in all our effulgent oneness.

When we find help from others we might notice our full healing *requires* our giving in return. Indeed, Aristotle taught that it is the very nature of goodness to spread itself around—and it does so automatically. This natural generosity may apply also to a new life-changing insight, an epiphany, the resolution of a long-standing problem. We have received a grace, and that grace wants to come through us to others. Thus what we have received makes us into assisting forces to others. When we find the pearl of great price we show it to everyone. When we open a door we feel moved to invite others to look in. What we receive we want to give.

This experience has a direct impact on motivation in one's work. Here is an example: a writer or artist has found or done something that seems really wonderful. This creative person sets up a website but it is not for self-promotion. It is to share good news with the world. The primary motivation is joy, not profit, though profit may be part of the also-welcome result.

The founder of Alcoholics Anonymous, Bill Wilson, discovered this important insight about giving: He relates that one night in Akron, he realized that the only way to help himself deal with his alcoholism was to try to help other alcoholics. His story demonstrates how becoming an assisting force toward those who need healing fosters a healing in ourselves. We see this concept in the twelfth step of the Alcoholics Anonymous program: "Having had a spiritual awakening as the result of these Steps, we tried to carry this message to alcoholics, and to practice these principles in all our affairs." The "awakening" also changes how people pray according to the book, *Alcoholics Anonymous*: "Never was I to pray for myself, except as my requests bore on my usefulness to others. Then only might I expect to receive." Loving-kindness changes prayer—and us—from "just for me" to "for me and all of us."

Finally, society itself can be a fellowship of assisting forces. Fellow citizens can be allies, a kinship we all so desperately need in today's world. Such solidarity happens when we let go of division while respecting diversity. We also can let go of a narcissistic focus in favor of a caring, committed connection to one another. Walt Whitman wrote about this opportunity and its archetypal quality in "To the East and to the West": "I believe the main purport of these States is to found a superb friendship, exaltè, previously unknown, / Because I perceive it waits, and has been always waiting, latent in all men."

THOSE WHO FAIL US

It may happen that we can no longer trust those who helped us before because they are not coming through as they used to—or worse, they have turned against us. What formerly sustained us has deserted us. Assisting forces have become afflicting forces. When those we thought were trusted allies fail us, we experience more than a disappointment. The loss can register in us as a trauma, since it is a break in trust—the central cause of all trauma. Deep trauma occurs when our whole body has believed others would be there for us as reliable assisting forces—and then one day they are not.

Using childhood abuse as an example, we can say that our parents hitting us was not the cause of our trauma but only a catalyst. The real trauma was the demolition of our innocent trust. Our parents caressed us at first and then turned on us. Later in life, betrayal by someone we trusted as an ally retraumatizes us if the betrayal is reminiscent of a sequence familiar from childhood. That is the moment of stark aloneness, which shatters our trusting heart. Yet a wonderful given of life abides and gives us hope: hearts that can be broken can be mended too.

For the sake of clarity, let's distinguish between child and adult trusting. In very early life children trust implicitly. Mature adults trust only when there is consistent evidence that the other person is indeed reliable. A child's loss of trust leads to an inability to trust others later, either partially or fully. The inability to trust can stay that way or, with work, the ability to trust might eventually be restored. Usually therapy will be necessary.

Now let's use the example of a breakdown of trust within an adult intimate relationship. A partner's loss of trust can be weathered and the trust can even be rebuilt. Our work will be to show our feeling response to the break in trust—to grieve it and open a dialogue, if the other is willing. Partners will look together at what happened. Each person will take responsibility for his or her part in the breakdown. Amends—making up for our offense—can follow, with new closeness as a result. This experience rebuilds our wounded capacity to trust. We let go of resentment, ill-will, and the need to retaliate—that is, we forgive.

We can't make ourselves forgive, but forgiveness can *happen* in that letting go. Most importantly, we notice we can trust ourselves more too. Then we realize that trusting ourselves was always the base camp, the starting point: we trust ourselves to receive trustworthiness with gratitude, and we handle betrayal with integrity and without retaliation. In both childhood and adulthood, beginning with self-trust is the best path to this healthy way of trusting others. We build support of ourselves from within, and only then from around us.[*]

ARTS AND ARTISTS

The "muse" of inspiration is the assisting force of the artist. Art in any form is an enduring ally to the human soul, both to the artist and to the observer: "Thou shalt remain . . . a friend to man," John Keats declares of the enigmatic Grecian urn, an object that speaks directly to the poet of truth and beauty.

To appreciate the arts is often considered integral to being a "cultured" person. Such a person is likely conversant with the riches of music, art, literature, and philosophy. They add a particular dimension to life that is impossible to find elsewhere. Those who appreciate the arts in this way would argue that Mozart was not just composing music for money; he was showing us the power of music to activate a region of our soul that could not locate its full territory otherwise. (In his 1697 tragedy *The Mourning Bride,* the playwright William Congreve offers the immortal lines that represent music as an ageless assisting force that is deeply therapeutic: "Music has charms to sooth a savage breast, / To soften rocks, or bend a knotted oak.")

For many such cultured persons, it's clear that a life without Rembrandt or Michelangelo would be less meaningful and enlivening—evolved minds, bodies, and imaginations could not be satisfied in a world without these masters. Indeed, it might seem that without Michelangelo's *Pietà* we would never have peered so far into the depths of human grief. Without Emily Dickinson how would we have known there were feelings that, unlike Rumpelstiltskin, could not be named? Nor was Dostoyevsky just telling a

[*] My book *Daring to Trust: Opening Ourselves to Real Love and Intimacy* (Shambhala, 2010) may help if you want more on this topic.

story about fathers and sons in *The Brothers Karamazov*. He was pointing to angles of feeling that we might not have reached into and so understand more about our own childhood home.

References to literature remind us of how books can be exceptionally delightful assisting forces, and indeed can be our companions through life. We booklovers loved having books read to us (and probably still do). We love reading books, we love owning them, we love how they feel to the touch and even how they smell. Books have helped us grow not only in vocabulary but in grasping how words are significant and impactful in a human life.

Books are allies who never leave us. They come to us from a long line of wise and imaginative guides. Indeed, books are assisting forces from assisting forces. Books tell us memorable stories that are about other people but they are also about ourselves— our dreams, our potentials, our deepest needs and longings. We may have books we will discard or give away—these have been our temporary assisting forces. Some we will never give away— they are our lifelong assisting forces. Books become important to us not only because of the topics that fascinate us and the authors we admire but also because the books we love have become representative of ourselves. We can't imagine life without them, because they are woven so deeply into the fabric of who we are. Books accompany us through every phase of life, beginning with Dick and Jane. Over the years we continue to discover new characters who keep us company, excite our ambitions, guide us onto surprising paths, steer us spiritually, get us through a lonely night, become our trusted comforters, become our necessary challengers. We will never know to what extent the ways we think and act have been influenced by the books we have read and cherished. Those cherished books may become worn and tattered, but they don't die; they outlive us, dog-ears and all. And perhaps our heirs will hold on to them as a way of not letting us ever fully go.

ANIMALS

In the shamanistic view, there are specific animals associated with each of us—animal energies within us. We can trust these "power animals" to increase our powers of courage and caution in the jungle of life, especially when we confront afflicting forces. Various animal spirits also endow us with their own forms of wisdom: thus the falcon flies us into falcon wisdom; the lion roars us lion wisdom; the hummingbird hums us hummingbird wisdom. Joseph Campbell helped us see that in many traditions an animal can be viewed as a shaman, a guardian, a herald of warning, a source of protection.

The word "totem" is a term used in tribal religions. It refers to a spiritual being, object, animal, or symbol that represents—and protects—a group of people such as a family, clan, or tribe. Nowadays too, people still think of animals as particularly important as spiritual allies. In fact, Carl Jung said that when we become more spiritually aware "an animal appears," whether in our daytime world or in a dream.

We have all enjoyed stories in which an animal comes to the aid of humans. A raven was said to have brought bread daily to St. Antony after the Egyptian monastic retreated to the desert. Dolphins have gained the appellation "friends of humans" for the innumerable examples of how they have helped us, including saving people at sea. Egyptian and Hindu gods are often part animal. Helpful animals abound in fables and fairy tales, such as the forest animals who help Snow White find solace and the cricket who tries to help Pinocchio obey his conscience. In Lewis Carroll's famous novel for children, a rabbit, a caterpillar, and a Cheshire cat help the heroine Alice look more perspicaciously into herself during her adventures in Wonderland. A brief look at the internet shows us myriad examples of how animals come to the aid of one another and of humans on a daily basis. Animals show us that alliance and assistance are *instinctive*.

Pets are an obvious example of animals as allies. A horse that has become very important to us is not just about assistance in getting from one place to another but about a kind of accompaniment we find nowhere else. The family cat is not just with us for her mousing skills. She brings a warm presence that is sorely missed when she is gone. Our love of dogs certainly includes the sense of them as allies—we even refer to them as "man's best friend." A beloved dog is not just a watchdog against intruders; he is a cherished companion watching out for your happiness and ending your isolation. He has transcended dog-ness in significance: he is more than an "animal" to you—and no one can convince you otherwise. We believe in the unique significance of our pets in our lives because we experience it daily.

Sometimes, the animal ally may appear in our inner world. In the Harry Potter stories, for instance, we meet the "Patronus," Harry's guardian spirit. He appears most splendidly as a white stag, thus an animal spirit. He can be conjured by magic but he can also simply show up when needed—as spiritual assisting forces often do. The word *patronus* is Latin for "patron," another reference to a guiding assisting force. In an archetypal story the figures are not simply "imaginary"—Jungian thought refers to them as "imaginal," meaning they are real at a deeper level than sense experience can capture or grasp. In stories that matter to us, we are meeting up with what life and we are *really* about.

THINGS

Throughout the ages people have relied on special objects to aid them when they find themselves caught in taxing or intimidating predicaments. Examples of these in stories are charms, amulets, elixirs, potions, magic lamps, gems, shields, special weapons, or guiding stars. There is also the *vademecum*—Latin for "go with me"—which refers to an item we might carry around with us all the time, usually for comfort or for a sense of security. (Again we notice the word "with," so indicative of the assisting force archetype at work.) Thus we have created a companionship of person and thing.

A keepsake provides a sense of connection to our past. We might cherish a modest family heirloom more than any expensive possession. Mementos in our home have a value beyond money: they remind us of kindly faces from our childhood and keep those faces gazing back at us, canceling the mind's partition of past from present, death from life. Mother's teapot, the one we saw so often on the table as she sat quietly late afternoons, the one she inherited from her mother, left to us when she died, is *more than* just a teapot now.

As we keep seeing, the words "more than" indicate transcendence, the essential quality of a *spiritual* reality. There is more in our cherished teapot than what meets anyone else's eye. It is a way of having her quiet caring energy with us again in the here and now. The meaning the teapot carries for us will not be felt by a stranger who comes upon it. To him it is only a container for tea. To us it has companionable significance at a transcendent level and it betokens an alliance unending.

To a person of faith, something will have a meaning beyond simple appearances, but to a nonbeliever, a religious object is just an object. To a believing person, certain objects offer a promise of heavenly companionship. Thus bread and wine in a religious context are more than food for the body; they are spiritually nurturant. To a Buddhist, a stick of incense is a sacred and purifying offering to Buddha—but to someone else the incense is not laden with any meaning other than its emitting of an exotic fragrance.

"Magic," as found in amulets and potions, is the fairy-tale version of what in spiritual consciousness is honored as "the transcendent." Thus, in *The Wizard of* Oz, the ruby slippers are more than footwear for Dorothy; and in the tale of "Jack and the

Beanstalk," the beans are more than beans in the hand of Jack. These items transcend the dictionary's limited definitions. They enhance the powers of those who have them—or rather, the items show the powers that were awaiting their turn to bloom.

NATURE

In *Walden*, Henry David Thoreau recorded his sense that "every little pine needle expanded and swelled with sympathy and befriended me. I was so distinctly made aware of the presence of something kindred to me, that I thought no place could ever be strange to me again." Is nature a friendly ally or indifferent to our survival? It is true that nature is not friendly in the sense of being interventionist. She will not prevent us from falling off a cliff. But nature does equip us to be careful on cliffs. Our legs and feet resonate with cautionary tingling as our bodies near a perilous edge. Nature has thus endowed us with an innate awareness of danger and with the motor ability to practice caution. These nature-given skills are certainly forms of friendliness toward our survival.

Another example of nature's friendliness is in the fact that we have been endowed with self-healing powers. We have a body that does not bleed to death when we cut our finger. Platelets come to the rescue and for the most part we easily survive.

Ultimately however, nature's superb way of being an ally is to be *hospitable*. She gives us a home replete with oxygen, light, water, fire, rich earth. "Will we be friendly to nature?" is the more pressing question nowadays. She is an impeccable host, but we are less than ideal guests. When our love of nature as an assisting force grows, it opens us to ecological consciousness and commitment to action to preserve the planet—yet another ally. In this challenge we are being invited to return the favor and be the allies of Mother Earth. How ironic that in these days, the archetype of the nurturer, nature, needs nurturance from us—and so many disregard nature's bid.

Throughout the ages, people have certainly found comfort in nature. William James, in *The Varieties of Religious Experience*, notes that "we all have moments when the universal life seems to wrap us round with friendliness." This comfort can indeed feel like being *held*—what we longed for not only in childhood but also long for now. Helen Keller reported that she could *feel* moonlight; it was *with* her. She transcended blindness, or rather, the ally moon did it for her. Here in California, I notice that the redwood trees provide a sense of accompaniment. They are not just standing there; they are standing alongside us, around us, over us, with us. Their presence feels like a promise that we will never be alone.

Spirituality is contact and communion with the *more* in all that is, and nature is where the "more" comes through to us so translucently. What strikes us with awe in the natural world shows us that it has more meaning than what it is described as in a science book. What intrigues us in nature calls to us, points a way, shows us why we are here, alerts us to alliances. In fact, all the things we love in nature mirror something spiritually alive in ourselves. The sky itself is a mirror of our soul's infinite extent. In ancient Egypt, the mother goddess Isis promised the pharaoh, Seti I, "I will give you the lifespan of the sky." In spiritual consciousness, the divine mother promises that same sky legacy to all of us. Can I become conscious of the vast scope of my higher Self, universe-sized? Such consciousness turns out to be a way the entire universe becomes present in us.

The word "universe" comes from a Latin root that means "the oneness that is ever turning." Nature is not static. Like ourselves, it is ever-evolving, ever-expanding. We evolve best when we join it in its endlessly creative impulse and its willingness to change.

Places, both nature-made and human-made, can also be assisting forces. All through the ages people have gone to the woods for solace, to a spring for healing. "Perhaps / The truth depends on a walk around a lake," wrote Wallace Stevens. Shrines in all traditions are located in places of natural beauty. These are places ever inviting us to what really matters at a soulful level.

I have noticed myself needing literally to sit on the ground at times in life when I am in deep distress or terror. I feel that only there can I become psychically grounded. And of course, I will go into the ground as a "final resting place" after I die. That ground is the one Buddha touched when he was asked who he was.

A WEEK OF PRACTICE

As a practice for enhancing our communion with nature, we can work with quotations about nature's glittering possibilities.

Read one of these quotations on each day of a week, copy it out in your own handwriting, and post it where you can see it throughout the day. You may also choose to rewrite it in your own words. Ponder it and record your ruminations. Then create an affirmation that shows how the quotation can activate itself in your here-and-now life. Finally, if it seems relevant or useful to you, write a heartful reply to any or all of the three questions following each quotation. Be sure to write in a free-flow, expansive style, not simply in one-sentence replies.

Sunday

I love the woods, particularly around the hermitage. I know every tree, every animal, every bird.

—Thomas Merton, *Learning to Love*

What will I allow to open in me when I find myself again alone in nature?

How can I encounter a tree or animal or bird and feel it as a spiritual emissary with a message meant for me?

What need or longing of mine is being fulfilled when I am in my favorite place in nature?

Monday

Walking, I can almost hear the redwoods beating. And the oceans are above me here, rolling clouds, heavy and dark. It is winter and there is smoke from the fires. It is a world of elemental attention, of all things working together, listening to what speaks in the blood. Whichever road I follow, I walk in the land of many gods, and they love and eat one another. Suddenly all my ancestors are behind me. Be still, they say. Watch and listen. You are the result of the love of thousands.

—Linda Hogan, *Dwellings:*
A Spiritual History of the Living World

How can I show gratitude for what nature offers me each day?

What will it take for me to appreciate that the things in the natural world are making a bid for my genuine caring about the planet?

How can I feel deep within myself that I am wrapped in friendliness by the natural things around me?

Tuesday

The incommunicable trees begin to persuade us to live with them, and quit our life of solemn trifles

—Ralph Waldo Emerson, "Nature"

Something in the rustling of the leaves is singing to me and wants me to join in. Can I agree to join into that magnificent harmony?

Can I commit myself to sitting mindfully under a tree more often and notice how much richer that can be than sitting on the sofa at home?

How is a tree a poem and can I dare write one?

Wednesday

Eventually I began to appreciate—I don't say this lightly—that the great black oaks knew me. I don't mean they knew me as myself and not another—that kind of individualism was not in the air, but that they recognized and responded to my presence, and to my mood. They began to offer, or I began to feel them offer, their serene greeting. It was like a quick change of temperature, a warm and comfortable flush, faint yet palpable, as I walked toward them and beneath their outflowing branches.

—Mary Oliver: *Winter Hours: Prose,*
Prose Poems, and Poems

What greets me in nature and wants to take my hand in a mystical marriage?

Can I let myself believe that nature knows me more deeply than some people do?

What does my presence in nature say and what is nature saying back to me?

Thursday

It is a spiritual victory to let go of a dualistic view of nature: The rivers flow not past us, but through us; the sun shines not on us, but in us.

—John Muir, "Mountain Thoughts"

How can I let go of looking at natural things as only outside me rather than around and in me?

What can I do today or soon to contribute to ecological balance, to respond to global warming, to take a stand for the planet?

How can I let what flows out there flow in and through my body and my heart?

Friday

The mind that searches for contact with the Milky Way is the very mind of the Milky Way galaxy in search of its own depths.

—Brian Swimme and Thomas Berry, *The Universe Story*

How can I open to the mystical consciousness that sees all diversity as one?

How can I expand my heart-body-mind to go beyond my own concerns to a universal caring consciousness?

How shall I say yes to finding the same infinite reaches in myself that I see in the night sky?

Saturday

Relentlessly, wave swells roll in toward the shallows, rise high, break into foaming crests, and plunge onto the shore. Waves are born when winds create friction with the sea's surface and infuse it with energy. As waves near the shore, the rising slope of the bottom of the ocean forces them into crests, and then into breakers. Waves release enormous energy when they crash upon the shore. All life in the surf zone must be able either to hide or to hold on for dear life.

—sign at Patrick's Point in Humboldt, California

How can I say yes to the torrents and crashes of my life so that I come to trust a power that turns them all into opportunities for evolutionary growth?

What will it take for me to turn all the frictions in my relationships into a single energy of love?

As I let go of despair and division, how can I find in nature what Gerard Manley Hopkins called "the dearest freshness deep-down things"?

IMAGES

As mentioned earlier, another way to contact our inner spiritual allies is to peer into a world of images that takes us beyond our family album: we contain a vast library of myth and metaphors that keeps revealing us to ourselves. This interior library is the collective treasury of human wisdom, an ally to which all of us have welcome access. For instance, we can think about an image that moves us or that has appeared to us in a dream, and we can deepen and elaborate on that. If we contemplate a rose, we go deeper to see more than just what botany classifies it to be; an inner botanical garden will perhaps flower in us with personal and cosmic dimensions.

Jung wrote, "Our fate appears in our images. . . . Whoever speaks in primordial images . . . evokes in us all those beneficent forces that ever and anon have enabled humanity to find a refuge from every peril and to outlive the longest night." Thus, images can become refuges in hard times. Such connection to images is another way interior work reveals and evokes a sense of oneness with our human heritage. When we take heart from images and scenes from nature, we find dimensionality, a *temenos,* a sacred space around and within us. Our unconscious has potentials we may not have guessed were there. Therefore, allowing those potentials to arise into consciousness rounds us out as full versions of ourselves. The treasury of images in our collective imagination is our inheritance, one we can never spend entirely. We then ask ourselves: How am I part of a larger picture than the ones in my family album?

The images that hold our attention or create awe in our souls are personal assisting forces. They reflect and evoke our own lively energy, whatever it is in us that is ready to awaken the sleeping giant, psyche. They declare our calling, what we are here to be and do. These are also some of the ways that meanings come through to us. To gaze, then, with awe, at an image is to evince from it the deep reality it signifies.

Attention is thus the key to enlisting allied powers. As an example, at healing shrines we focus on the energy there and we may experience a new integration of our bodies and hearts. Such an integration can also happen as we show reverence to an icon, a *thangka*, or any spiritually meaningful image. They can open to us and thereby become assisting forces.

From a religious perspective, an icon can help us contact our interior assisting forces. We can consider an icon depicting a saint to be moving in two directions: we look at the saint and she looks back at us. Thus an icon can become a catalyst to what Martin Buber would term an "I-and-Thou" encounter. A photograph is simply an object we look at. But an image of a revered icon involves a meeting between ourselves as we seem to be and ourselves as who we really are. After all, from a spiritual perspective, we are all saints in fledgling states. An icon is not an object but a mirror of our own spiritual identity. All that stands in the way of acknowledging this saintly identity is our self-doubt, a hindrance to our wholeness. As we strive for wholeness, saints we venerate and heroic people we admire can be assisting forces to us: the New Testament book of Hebrews urges, "Since we are surrounded by such a great cloud of witnesses, let us throw off everything that hinders."

In Buddhism, the equivalent of an icon for stirring devotion is a thangka—a Tibetan Buddhist image on cloth or parchment showing a Buddha, a bodhisattva, or a scene from Buddha's life. There is usually one central enlightened figure and others around him or her. Some thangkas are poster-size and occupy a place of honor in a home or temple. Thangkas are mirrors revealing our Buddha nature and calling us to the wisdom and compassion in our Buddha nature. A thangka is an object of reverence and meditation that calls us to the Dharma, the enlightened teachings.

In another context, there may also be an image, statue, or figurine of our own that we treasure. We bring it with us—it comes with us—from house to house when we move. Indeed, we would not feel we were truly at home without it. That object is *accompanying* us and is hence an example of an assisting force. In fact, anything we cherish and keep in our possession is accompanying us each day, reminding us we live not alone but *with*.

Some images stabilize and sustain us when we feel ourselves adrift from our moorings. Even pictures we have drawn or have chosen for our walls or desk may have allies significant for us. In my own experience, I have a collection of images that are meaningful to me. When I look at them in difficult times I notice I become more confident that I can handle whatever is happening—or may happen. I recommend this practice as a pathway to self-soothing.

A specific image that works along these lines is a *mandala*, the Sanskrit word for circle. A mandala is usually a circular or square design containing symbols in an elaborate pattern that represent the spiritual journey. Practitioners focus their attention on the mandala as a form of or entry into meditation. The arc of attention is meant to move from the outer rim of the mandala to its center. In fact, contemplation of a mandala centers those who gaze into it.

To demonstrate impermanence, a concept central to Buddhist teaching, Buddhist monks sometimes create sand mandalas— developed a few grains at a time in painstaking detail and using a variety of colors. As soon as they have completed this tedious and intricate task, the monks destroy the mandala, sweeping the sand back into a pile. Then another mandala can take shape, showing how impermanence is connected to renewal.

Jung noted that mandala-like images appear in most religious traditions—the rose window of a cathedral being a prime example. In *Memories, Dreams, Reflections*, Jung's autobiography, he shared how working with a mandala can be a valuable spiritual practice: "I sketched every morning in a notebook a small circular drawing . . . which seemed to correspond to my inner situation at the time," he writes. From Jung's point of view a mandala depicts the divine presence abiding at the center of every human psyche:

"Only gradually did I discover what the mandala really is," he notes—he determined that it represented "the Self, the wholeness of the personality, which if all goes well is harmonious." The mandala is a mirror image of the wholeness stably residing in our interior life, no matter how shaky our conscious life may have become.

In his book *Kindness, Clarity, and Insight,* the Fourteenth Dalai Lama expands on what this can look like in practice: "The main technique is for one consciousness to contain the two factors of observing a mandala circle of deities and simultaneously of realizing their emptiness of inherent existence. In this way, the vast, the appearance of deities, and the profound, the realization of suchness, are complete in one consciousness."

The mandala mirrors the structure and riches of the unconscious, of those layers of memories and images that keep deepening in significance in the course of life. A mandala configures the layers into a unity. In spiritual awareness that is exactly what exploring our inner life is meant for: we find an ultimate unity in ourselves, among one another, and with the entire cosmos. In fact, that unity is the origin and destiny of all that is. A mandala is a portrait of that marvelously vast and frontierless reality. Any person can say, "All of me is a mandala made flesh."

I have a unique destiny: to display here and now the timeless mandala of love that is in me.

This is why I was given a lifetime.

I trust that whatever happens to me is part of how my destiny of love unfolds, nothing to fear or regret.

I trust that nothing that happens to me can cancel my capacity to go on loving.

4 WHEN INTIMATE PARTNERS ARE INTIMATE ALLIES

Human nature will not easily find a helper better than love.
—Plato, *The Symposium*

"You are as prone to love as the sun to shine. Love is the true means by which the world is enjoyed: our love for others and their love for us," proclaimed the metaphysical poet Thomas Traherne in his *Centuries of Meditations*. "If we cannot be satisfied by love, we cannot be satisfied at all. Never was anything in this world loved too much . . . but only in too short a measure." Walking hand in hand, arm in arm, heart to heart, a loving relationship can be a partnership of allies. A partner who loves us in full measure is an ally in accord with phrases and images that first appeared in our introduction:

There—or here—for me
Comes through for me
In my corner
On my team
Supports me
Has my back
Props me up

Encourages the best in me
Backs me up
Always stands up for me
Believes in me
At my side

A bond of love includes all of these gifts, mutually given and received. Authentic intimacy happens when love includes alliance and two partners act as assisting forces of one another.

An essential benefit of an assisting force in any relationship is a sense of empowerment-by-alliance as we face a crisis: "I can get through this with you at my side." Sometimes all we need is someone who shows up, who sits beside us with a hand in ours. An ally can also help us by being more than that.

- Sometimes we need someone behind us, backing us up.
- Sometimes we need someone going to bat for us.
- Sometimes we need someone stepping in for us—for instance, we might need someone in our corner as we battle with people who treat us unjustly.

The partner who is an ally is in tune with what we need. Such a partner

- knows what we are going through,
- sees us through a conflict,
- stays with us as we go through a hard time, and
- stays with us through thick and thin.

A partner who is a friend and ally is also genuinely delighted about our growth, our progress, our achievements. Such a person is not envious of our good fortune and is never competing with us or one-upping us. We appreciate and trust the partner who wants only the best for us. We can tell when someone is glad we are prospering, happy about our happiness. In Buddhism, joy at another's good fortune is a quality of enlightenment.

THE FIVE A'S

The caring, committed connection of intimate love is characterized by "five A's": attention or attentiveness, affection, appreciation, acceptance, and allowing. Each of us was born with the capacity to give and receive these five A's. They are faculties in every psyche, but they may have been damaged in childhood or in past relationships. Trauma, betrayal, or abuse may have hobbled us in walking love's labyrinthine path. Then it will be hard to show the five A's to others—that is, it will be hard to act as an ally. It may also be difficult to receive the five A's, if our trust in those who paraded themselves as allies was betrayed.

Our work, our life challenge, is to show our love, to activate or reanimate our five capacities of love so that they become daily practices. In fact, even without fully resolving our issues, we can simply practice attentiveness, affection, appreciation, acceptance, and allowing—it does not matter whether or not we feel psychologically healthy enough to give or receive them. We limp but walk on anyway—recognizing that practice is all that is asked of us, not perfection.

Intimacy happens when partners show these five A's mutually and reliably. The score does not have to be even or perfect. Love is happening when these five A's are being expressed *in good-enough ways most of the time with a back-and-forth style*. No partner can be expected to fulfill all five A's all the time. In fact, a mature adult would not want a partner who was like that—too close for comfort. A mature adult has built a cohort of inner and outer allies. A partner is then a primary needed reinforcement, not a do-it-all-for-me or the-only-one-I-turn-to. Twenty-five percent of need fulfillment is all that an adult would ask of any one person. More is too much. Less is not enough.

Each of these A's is a form of alliance, an assisting force in a love relationship:

- Attentiveness: we notice and attune to one another's words, needs, and feelings with an alert awareness of body language even when the words are not explicit.
- Affection: we show our loving connection in physical ways and yet always with respect for one another's boundaries. We speak and act with warmth and tender kindliness, frequently saying "I love you."
- Appreciation: we show respect and we do not take one another for granted but express gratitude for all we do for or mean to one another.
- Acceptance: we accept each other as each of us is not as we expect one another to be, and only from that platform can we show up as allies to one another.
- Allowing: we are available to be of help but always with respect for one another's autonomy, boundaries, and freedom to make the choices that reflect one another's own deepest needs, values, and wishes.

These five A's add up to deep presence. We are really present to others when we are showing attention, affection, appreciation, acceptance, allowing. Others are present to us when they are doing the same for us. Such presence is the essence, origin, and goal of companionship.

Each *A* we ask for represents a need we are willing to reveal and be vulnerable enough to admit having. A truly reliable partner *welcomes* needs from the other rather than finding them a burden or running from them. A need is a bid for alliance, a call for solidarity. Being present to a need, fulfilling it if possible, is the style of an assisting force. Indeed, the allowing feature of the five A's includes welcoming needs as legitimate. In addition, we not only allow, we appreciate—that is, value—every mood and feeling of our partner as an invitation into new rooms in his or her or their psyche. Love introduces us to one another's spacious and surely surprising inner world. And then we ask, "Did my parents offer that to me? Does my partner do that? Do I do that?"

A relationship in which the five A's are mutually given creates a "holding environment," in which partners feel affirmed as they are. In a holding environment, we fully trust that we can be ourselves, wounds and all. We can say anything about our shames or struggles and trust we will not be thought less of or turned away. We can display our shadow side, admit our faults, and trust that we will still be loved. We see that as an ally our partner will not judge us as wrong or bad but assist us toward more effective ways of interacting. Our faults are then not sources of shame. They are indicators of the need for better social skills, for more wisdom in our choices, for more depth in how we show our love.

We will always have to beware of a shaming voice inside ourselves—beware of the inner critic, that strict sergeant of self-abnegation who delights in putting us down and shaming us, especially when we are at a low ebb in our lives. We fall for the inner critic's story when we buy into his fraudulent "shoulds." The inner critic, like any fear of being ourselves, is a bully, a terrorist looking for our weak spot, exploiting our deepest self-doubts and insecurities about our adequacy. If only we could see that the inner critic has no real authority but in fact is only a paper tiger.

Taking pride in being ourselves, however daunting to us, can actually lead to a release from the grip of our inner critic:

- We make the choices that represent our own deepest needs, values, and wishes, not those of others.
- We show ourselves to others in transparent ways with no fear of letting them see our inadequacies.
- With self-compassion we realize that some of the thoughts and actions we don't like in ourselves are based on old habits and don't reflect who we are now.

- We act with integrity and loving-kindness.
- We come to see the things that have happened in our relationships as simple facts, not reasons for blame of others or shame about ourselves.
- We love having friends and allies but trust we can still thrive if they fail us.
- We can relate to our brokenness with self-compassion rather than let it decimate our self-esteem. To say there is "God within" or that "we all have Buddha nature" means that our inner brokenness can hold both God and enlightenment. It is only our resistance to our full shadow self that blocks our access to our divine or enlightened grandeur.

We have evidence that relationships, both intimate and friendly, promote not only happiness—a release from our inner critic and growth in knowing ourselves and one another—but they also promote optimal physical well-being. Dean Ornish, in *Love and Survival: The Scientific Basis for the Healing Power of Intimacy,* shows that loving connectedness has a directly positive effect on our health: "Although diet, blood pressure, and other risk factors play an important role in developing heart disease and angina, these factors can be significantly moderated by a loving relationship. . . . Most scientific studies have demonstrated the extraordinarily powerful role of love and relationships in determining health and illness."

We could say our solidarity with others keeps us alive. When we make it a point to work things out with our partner so love and trust can flourish, when we stay in touch with friends and make time to be with them, we are not just being good partners and friends. We are not just making our life easier. We are helping one another make our lives last longer. Life extension is not our motive, but it is quite a desirable effect.

THE PHASES OF ROMANCE, CONFLICT, AND COMMITMENT

Most successful relationships go through three stages: romance, conflict, commitment. (Relationships that do not work out usually end in the conflict stage, often with grudges in its wake.)

High Romance

We usually begin relating to someone with romantic feelings that lead to what blooms into "high" romance. "High" is an apt word, since we are on a hormonal "high" when our romance is at full speed. At this stage, we experience "chemistry" with one another. "Chemistry" refers to an exciting combination of dopamine—the reward hormone—and oxytocin—the warm-cuddly hormone. Those hormones give pleasure and provide a sense of safety and security. We are in one another's thoughts all the time and love being close, even clinging, to one another; we are erotic allies joined at the hip. We can enjoy all of this problem-free for as long as it lasts: Romance is an appropriate beginning for any intimate relationship. It is also Mother Nature's way of making sure the human race will be propagated.

There are, however, two issues we may not be noticing. One is that high romance is not sustainable. Our bodies can't handle so much extreme hormonal excretion. The other is that in romance we do not clearly see who our partner really is. We are looking at our own projection of the "perfect one for me." We are looking at our own lifelong longing for love mirrored in the face we have put on our beloved. Our partner is doing the same with us. We can't see a real other until all that fantasy-driven excitement subsides. Only then do we see the clay feet, the shadow side, the limitations—observations that usher in the next phase of an intimate relationship. Gradually we come back from high romance to baseline. That can happen while romantic feelings continue but now in a quiet, more even-keeled way. The relationship is still, in that instance, oxytocin-rich, but it is not overdone as it was at first. As partners we see each other more clearly, but still not fully. For that, we will need a few fights.

Conflict

Conflict is the second phase of most relationships. We see the unseemly side of one another. We find ourselves struggling as the egos that used to pet one another now scrape one another. We disagree about things that were easy to agree on before. When "the thrill is gone," we find intolerable the very quirks that were so endearing in the romance phase. And then our question may be "Is that all there is?"

A partner who is a genuine ally will want to work through conflicts—rather than hold grudges or retaliate, which are two sure-fire ways to cancel alliance. An ally partner is someone who does all it takes to convey the bond into its next phase, commitment. This work takes "deepening through conflict." Yes, we can form a deeper bond through our conflicts. How can this happen? We can mutually engage in a three-part program in the face of conflicts: (1) addressing, (2) processing, and (3) resolving our issues.

The first part of constructive conflict in an intimate relationship is *addressing*. We acknowledge that there is a problem—always the first step toward resolving any issue. We admit our concern or distress to ourselves and then to our partner. We call the problem by name and speak it aloud with no blame or shame. We express our concerns using "I" statements not "you" statements, since that imputes fault. We do not tell other people what they are feeling. We ask and listen.

Implicit in the word "addressing" is moving beyond one's own projections in order to look directly at one another and at whatever is happening between us. Of course, we don't trust our vision or version of what we see. We keep checking in with one another about whether we got it right. This exploration may require help from a neutral third party such as a therapist. We might share our perceptions with a wise friend—that is, an ally of the relationship, rather than of either partner's ego.

The second part of constructive conflict in an intimate relationship is *processing*. To process an experience is first of all to share and show our feelings. We show feelings openly and take full responsibility for them. When we bottle our own feelings up we lose our chance to resolve them. Hiding our feelings is a form of distancing—something else to look into. We ask, "What agenda do I have? Am I showing up in this relationship to increase closeness or to increase distance?" True closeness can only happen when we share what we are feeling, even about the elephant in the room.

The next element of processing involves looking at how we are being emotionally provoked, or triggered. We let ourselves see what our triggers and feelings are based on. We then may see more clearly what really motivates how we feel, act, or react. We especially notice if we are overreacting, because a feature of being triggered is that we might interpret what people say and do in a skewed way. For instance, if we are triggered by being criticized, we might interpret an ordinary question as criticism. As we continue in our practice of processing, we come to appreciate those who trigger us because they show us what is happening in us and what we may have to work on in ourselves

In my 2019 book *Triggers: How We Can Stop Reacting and Start Healing*, I describe how we can link triggers that are affecting us in the present to one or more of three possible sources: the shadow, the ego, or an earlier life issue. The first source, the *shadow*, refers to aspects of ourselves that we are unconscious of but that we might now be projecting onto a partner. We see in what upsets us about others exactly what we need to confront in ourselves: long-occluded attitudes, feelings, and behaviors. We might be unaware, for instance, that we are controlling and manipulative—but we see that quality quite clearly in our partner. We are actually looking at our own disavowed, repressed traits.

A second source of triggers is *ego*. We may feel ego indignation that someone dared to cross us, humble us, call us out on something. Our pride has been hurt. This pride is the inflated, arrogant ego that believes itself entitled to respect while not acknowledging that others need respect too and deserve it as much as we. The big ego is also highly vindictive. Revenge is its favorite sport, the one it most excels at. Since relationships can only thrive on forgiveness, retaliation kills our chances for happiness and intimacy.

When we retaliate in a relationship, we might ask ourselves if we are punishing a partner in the present for what a parent did to us in childhood. Our work is grieving and letting go of the past so that it no longer interrupts the present moment or makes a present partner take the role, unwittingly, of a character from long ago.

Another habit of ego is to enforce dependence. This kind of subjugation is not an alliance but a jurisdiction. When we really love someone we let that person be free. Our ego doesn't need to parade itself as essential to someone else's survival. Surely, we will have to cede every inch of ego turf if we are ever to love someone. Letting go of ego will feel like the lifting of a weight from our heart, a weight we have been carrying and adding to since ninth grade. When the self-entitled ego bites the dust from whence it came, we will no longer be using a relationship to gratify our ego. Instead, we will be dispossessing ourselves of ego to gratify the relationship. In other words, we will become a loving ally.

A final source of triggers is rooted in feelings connected to an *earlier life issue*. Things that trigger us in the present usually have a correspondence with something similar that happened in our past, either in other adult relationships or as far back as childhood. Our feelings may be repetitions of or expressions of trauma or they may indicate unfinished emotional business, now making a bid for completion. We may be finally showing to a partner something that was unsafe to show to a parent or former partner.

We may recall experiences of repression or inhibition in childhood or in adulthood. We felt it was *dangerous* to be who we were or show what we wanted or even what we loved. It may take us a while to realize that the experience of repression has actually impacted us as trauma. A clue to the presence of such trauma is how unsafe we may feel now as mature adults when who we really are is not supported by others—or worse, is used against us. To be "known" for who we truly are and loved for it is exhilarating. To be known and hated or shamed for it is terrifying. Another clue is being triggered into fear by things we see in the media (news items or a movie, for instance) that show people endangered or harmed because of who they are—and who they are is who we are.

Both of these examples are experiences of post—or ongoing—traumatic stress. We will need the assisting force of those who are like us, or who like us, to move beyond our traumatic fear reactions, especially the ones that come in flashbacks. When we feel shut down and find ourselves scared stiff by danger or threat coming at us, that reaction is not cowardice. It is the natural freeze response from a post-traumatic stress disorder. The words in this paragraph can themselves be our assisting forces on the path to freedom from any or every fear.

The territory of "what is safe to show" about who we are is without limit when a relationship is built on trust. We know our partner is an ally when we can be ourselves, reveal our deepest needs and longings, display our true identity, stand nakedly as ourselves without shame or inhibition. When who we are evokes a frown, we are not with an ally. Then we might say what the shy and fig-leafed Adam mumbled to God in Eden: "I was afraid because I was naked, so I hid myself." Adam's words express the most heartbreaking of all our human conundrums: when it is dangerous to be ourselves we wind up hiding our dazzling uniqueness—even from ourselves.

KOAN PRACTICE

One counterintuitive way to process conflict is to turn our problem into a question that can't be answered. This inversion is how a koan works in Buddhist tradition. A koan is a riddle that stumps the rational mind, and when asked to solve a koan we must move into a larger space than logic can measure or dare allow. The tightening style of linear thinking does not work in dealing with a koan. We have to embark on another way of knowing. This open way of thinking has much in common with reading a poem—it requires some comfortableness with uncertainty.

Take the following koan, which offers two choices, neither of which is acceptable: "How can I let go of control and not have everything fall apart?" The answer will not be choosing one over the other. We let go of having to choose. We simply sit between them. Then suddenly, as if from nowhere, we hear a voice in ourselves say, "I will let the chips fall where they may and then make the best of how they fall." Now we are arriving at a felicitous combination of apparent opposites. We have stepped out of the dilemma of either-or, and suddenly everything has settled into a whole new and unexpectedly satisfying configuration.

Another way to do this practice is to hold out our hands, palms up, and imagine holding the two contesting choices, one in each hand, without favoring either. When we hold opposites, granting equal hospitality to both, they are likely to become candidly communicative with one another. We listen in, and they find ways of shaking hands with one another. (Of course, some oppositions do not reconcile. In those cases, we simply hold them and accept that they are irreconcilable—at least for now.)

The third and final part of constructive conflict in an intimate relationship is *resolving*: To resolve a conflict in a relationship is to reach a mutually satisfactory outcome, one that leads us to a more productive way of interacting. For example, we resolve the issue of having hurt a partner's feelings by showing contriteness and receiving forgiveness. We then make an agreement to work with our aggression and show our feelings more skillfully. Our willingness to make and keep agreements is a necessary feature of resolving an issue—and it is a feature of authentic intimacy too.

The opposite of resolving is resenting, in which we hold things against one another openly or secretly, usually engaging in passive-aggressive behavior. We may hold on to a grudge, another gold-medaled sport of the ego. We keep revisiting our anger rather than expressing it and laying it to rest. We remain caught in the toils of fault and blame wherein no resolution is possible.

In an authentic resolution of an immediate conflict, we see our part in any contention and commit ourselves to do what it takes to avoid repeating it. We don't keep bringing it up or holding it against the other. We have moved from holding on to letting go— our hardest human task, as well as our path to ally intimacy.

At the end of a relationship we move on only when there is no more blame or need to retaliate in our hearts. All the past conflicts are truly past. They have become simply information that no longer triggers us. We don't feel the need to tell people how wrong our partner was. Calmly, we say only, "It didn't work out between us and now I hope we can become friends," or effective coparents, or whatever the desired outcome may be. We have flown from fault to fact. We have landed on the sublime plane of consciousness where all that matters is moving on with love.

There are times when no closure or resolution is possible, just our surrendering to the fact of stuckness and our need for help if we are ever to get through it. Sometimes—never really knowing what happened to us, feeling incomplete—being left with no resolution is all we come up with. Help seems useless. Then our attitude of "yes to what is, as it is" assists us again.

Sometimes in a conflicted relationship we may know, deep-down, that it is not the time to break up but also not the time to make a full commitment. We are in-between. In that confusing logjam we have a third skillful alternative: we do all we can to get the relationship to work; we act as if we are totally committed even though we don't feel committed. When we engage in this both-feet-in practice we are guaranteed to wake up one morning and know whether it is time to stay or go. Putting our whole heart into staying shows us whether to stay put or step out.

An aside: We can observe that letting go proves its value in that it is also a form of accessing inner knowledge. Consider how often we can't think of a name or word no matter how hard we try—then we stop trying and it just comes to us shortly after, with no further effort needed. What a paradox: we let go to retrieve, turn away to locate, stop seeking to find. We ask: Dare I visit lands of paradox like those?

Commitment

After the whirl of high romance and the work of deepening through conflict, the third and final phase in establishing a relationship is making a commitment for a future together. This pledge of per-manence happens when conflicts are being cleared up more and more often by sincere addressing, processing, and resolving. Res-olution of a conflict evolves into an agreement, a plan to change something so that the bond can proceed more smoothly and more firmly too.

When this happens, and keeps happening, we know that we are in the commitment phase of our relationship. Conflicts still occur but no longer with the puffed-up bantam ego loudly crowing to win or be right. We will be, instead, finding it easier to let that need go. And best of all, we no longer believe anyone *has* to win or be right. We will feel such a relief in that "it doesn't really matter" moment. That relief is a clue that we are, at last, letting go of ego and all its dogged fears—that is, we are letting intimacy happen. We think, "As I access the tender vulnerability under every one of my fears I notice I am less afraid of closeness."

RELATIONSHIPS AS ASSISTING FORCES

Consider how each of the three features of working something out—addressing, processing, and resolving—shows up with respect to the assisting-force archetype in relationship.

- In the romance phase, the ally is a fun mate who strongly feels caring for and connection with us.
- In the conflict phase, we see whether our partner is an afflicting or assisting force, based on how conflicts are handled or not handled.
- In the commitment phase, there is no doubt we are with an ally and it feels like our alliance will last. Only a committed person can be a true assisting force in a relationship. Commitment here means that conflicts are indeed handled and the agreements that emerge from them are indeed kept.

A spiritually aware partnership in the commitment stage will usually open out into concern for the wider world. We will find ourselves involved in projects that contribute to the welfare of others and the planet too. This is what love looks like at high tide. It will not be the "high" in excited romance but the "high" in matured love.

It is in the commitment stage that we become wise enough to know whether marriage is right for us, if that is our goal. Marrying while in the heady romance phase can be a big mistake—most of us know someone who has found that out. In the romance stage we don't know if we are with someone who will be willing to work out conflicts or keep agreements or be trustworthy. We don't know if abuse will happen. We don't know if addiction will arise. We don't know if fidelity will be assured.

In other words, we don't know enough to make a lifetime vow; we know only enough to enjoy someone in the bedroom. And that is not a stable setting to start so intricate and fragile a lifetime enterprise. First we need some final reassurance that we have an emotionally healthy and trustworthy partner who will accompany us through life as an ongoing ally, and we look for qualities that will allow that relationship to happen:

Attunement

An ally attunes to us in an empathic way, deeply grasping what we are saying and feeling. Empathic attunement allows us to feel into someone else's experience or pain and then, through mirroring, show that we feel it too—we affirm, by word, touch, action, or gesture, that we understand it. Attunement includes the five A's:

- We pay *attention* to someone's words, needs, feelings, and longings at a feeling level.
- We *appreciate* and value someone's feelings, so we treat them with respect and not try to talk them out of them.
- We hold and stay with the other's concern or pain with comforting words and with physical *affection*, appropriate to the nature and ground rules of the relationship.
- We *accept* rather than reject the other person, making no attempts to make the other over in accord with our likes, demands, or expectations.
- We *allow* someone to be exactly who that someone is rather than trying to be in control of another person's behavior or choices. We are thereby doing what all allies do: honoring the other person's deepest needs, values, and wishes.

Cole Porter, in his song "In the Still of the Night," asks a poignant question that many of us have asked in our relationships:

"Do you love me as I love you?" We may expect the love between ourselves and our partner to be equal in how it is felt, in how it is shown. Sometimes we even demand that parity, or we feel unloved if it is not forthcoming. But a mature relationship is not about exact equivalence. It is about *acceptance* of others' limits and of their unique way of showing love compared to ours: "I want to accept your brand of love even though it is not the same as mine—though I can always ask for more as time goes by."

Regarding *allowing*, in spiritual maturity, our definition of control changes: we no longer view control in ego language—"I am in charge here"—but rather in sane-adult language—"I can handle what happens." We then step up to the plate and are ready to hear what an experience has come to teach us. We follow with whatever action gets us through the situation. This acceptance of reality is the healthy version of being in control.

Misattunements happen in all relationships. But in an atmosphere of mended failures—the only atmosphere in which love can thrive—we don't see misattunement to our feelings as a reason to blame the other. Instead, we note that our feeling or message seems to have been unperceived or misconstrued, and we ask for another chance to convey what we said or felt. We do this in a non-blaming way—for instance: "When I feel misattuned to, I am glad to explain what I feel again," or "When I misattune to you, I ask that you let me know so I can try again."

In a style so respectful, we come to see attuning as a skill that any of us can learn. It is the talent of an assisting force. Also, when we fail to attune to a partner's feeling, we might say, "I am not ashamed about this misattunement though I am sorry about it. I am learning the skill of attuning and will keep practicing. I do not offer perfection, only the sincerity of my ongoing intention and efforts, however inadequate or tardy."

If the assessment we are making is irrational, we use a different protocol when asking for attunement: we ask for a partner's *presence* while we do our own work on it. We do not ask for rescue from it. For instance, perhaps we suffer from intense jealousy, so we feel scared, even panicked, when our spouse has friendly contact with her ex-husband. She tells us there is no attraction left, no erotic component in her relating to him, and we know this is true but we still feel fear. We know this irrational jealousy is a common pattern for us and that freedom from it is our personal work. So we admit we are overreacting and ask her to hear about the paranoid shape our fear has taken.

We also bravely ask her not to keep reassuring us that she is no longer attracted to him. That only coddles our fear and does not help us get over it. A true ally and partner in relationship does not do that; she helps us face our fear, talk about it, and feel it, but she does not try to cancel it so we can feel better. (This portrayal might bring to mind a scene from the film *Ordinary People*: "Let me feel bad about this!" Timothy Hutton's character tells his psychiatrist, wanting an ally who does not to try to soothe him but only stay with him as he feels his pain fully.)

An ally who acts in this adult way helps us be adult too. In this situation, "adult" means letting go of jealousy that is not appropriate and letting go of whatever fear is interfering with healthy relating. In our dialogue we can admit our fear, acknowledge it as irrational, and even show it verbally and bodily in a way that is appropriate.

All our ally and partner has to do, all we ask her to do, is listen. She is attuning to how we are triggered but not jumping in to extricate us from our feelings. Standing by, an assisting-force style, is how she is helping us move through them. This kind of presence is the equivalent of physical holding. It applies not only to our experience of trauma or fear but also to grief or any feeling we find it hard to handle on our own.

A Capacity for Satisfaction

In some relationships we seek a partner who will make up for what we missed out on in childhood. An assisting force is not designed to do that for us. That would not be helping us acknowledge our actual need and it may be misdirecting it too. The need for one or more of the five A's in childhood can't be made up for by an adult partner because we were at a different developmental stage in childhood experience than we are now as adults. Furthermore, in early life we wanted and needed 100 percent attention, affection, appreciation, acceptance, allowing—but adults don't offer emotional support that way. They only offer moderate amounts, the adult dosage.

Our task instead is the personal work of grieving the lack of fulfillment of our early needs. Such grief is itself an assisting force in our psychological and spiritual task: our grief helps us let go of seeking things in our life that are gone and helps us open ourselves to what another adult can actually provide. It will be a caring, committed connection marked by the five A's in an adult-to-adult style—not a parent-to-child style. The adult style is "good enough" and "most of the time"—not perfect all the time. A partner who shows up this way is an ally of our development.

In embarking on a truly healthy relationship we are letting go of resentment about the holes in the past. We are not trying to fill those holes or find someone to fill them for us. We have acknowledged them, cried about them. We have let them become simply a part of our history—background, not interference. In other words, we have learned to walk safely on the moonscape of relationship, always a cratered land.

Insatiably wanting more and more from an adult partner is our clue that an original deprivation is still tugging at us and that it is still not fully grieved and let go of. That wanting more is, however, also a way of deflecting our grief. Only an embrace of our grief about our impoverished past can free us from our insatiability in the present. So we lose twice when we keep wanting more, rather than allowing ourselves to mourn the less and become open to a moderate fulfillment now. Only with this work on ourselves comes a capacity to be satisfied. That was the capacity that would have been installed in us in childhood if our needs had been met in a good-enough way.

Early deprivation disables our ability to be satisfied with the moderate dose of caring, committed connection that a healthy adult can give. Our need for more and more proof that we are loved, displayed too often compulsively, is how we tell the story of our empty childhood, how we let it be known today that we were hungry every day. But we no longer have to tell the story once we have let go of our umbrage about past deprivations and misattunements. We find that capacity when we grieve the past and let go of the resentments that cling to its memories.

A relationship in which one person can't give enough and the other can't get enough is agonizing indeed. The former is painfully codependent and the latter is painfully needy. We are allies to one another only when both of us have done the work of healing our own pasts. In other words, to be a truly assisting force in a relationship takes work on *ourselves*. We will ask, "Am I willing to roll up my ego-sleeves and give this a try?" And partners can act as allies by encouraging each other in facing exactly this challenge. Supporting our personal work is a loved task of a loving assisting force.

Closeness and Distance

In an allied, companionable relationship we do not fear healthy, intimate closeness. We do not find it smothering. Nor do we fear reasonable or occasional distance or see it as abandonment. Likewise, we are not in a relationship to stave off our own abandonment fears—rather, we cherish and value bonding with our partner both when we're together and when we're miles apart. If we do fear the healthy love we seek, however, it could be for any of the following reasons:

- We will have to be vulnerable and thereby not be in control.
- We will have to be open to another person's way of loving and thereby not be in control.
- We will be challenged to love unconditionally and thereby not be in control.

- We will have to let ourselves be seen just exactly as we are and that unmasking will be terrifying.

How ironic that our holding on to safety is really holding on to the fear!

Attachment theory holds that a partner can best be an ally and intimate companion in a secure bond. Such a partner will be reliably available and attuned. The insecure-anxious partner clings because of abandonment fears. The insecure-avoidant person runs away or distances because of the fear of being engulfed. The disorganized person cannot relate at all.

In *Deprivation and Delinquency*, the pioneering child psychiatrist D. W. Winnicott wrote, "Only if someone has her arms around the infant . . . can the I AM moment be endured, or rather, risked."* In other words, we gain from those who give us a go-ahead, permission to be who we really are. This permission happens in secure attachment, not only in childhood but also in adult relationships. It manifests in an ongoing attunement to our feelings, words, and needs and a willingness to show each other the five A's in a generous way:

- Attention: We turn toward one another with an engaged focus and remain present for as long as is needed.
- Affection: We show our love through touch and holding—a cradling of one another's bodies with simultaneous respect for one another's boundaries. Sex is then about deepening, enriching, and celebrating our bond rather than using one another. In addition, we never use sex as a weapon.

---

* Winnicott's philosophy parallels the assertion of Martin Buber that I quoted in the introduction: "A person wishes to be confirmed in his being by another person. . . . Secretly and bashfully, he watches for a Yes which allows him to be and which can come only from one human person to another. It is from one human being to another that the heavenly bread of self-being is passed." Both quotations suggest the connection between mirroring love and assisting force.

- Appreciation: We value one another as the primary assisting forces in one another's lives, with an ever-deepening gratitude.
- Acceptance: We fully embrace one another's personality traits, moods, limitations, gifts, and needs as totally okay with us and with no attempt to change one another. We are in love with the true self of another person, not the self we had hoped to find.
- Allowing: We respect one another's freedom and autonomy while honoring the ground rules of and boundaries in our relationship.

Picking Up the Pieces

We all have times in our lives when we fall apart, destabilize, dysregulate. The partner who can be there for us in those unkempt moments is a truly assisting force, our trusted accompanier. During this time we may not be able to fulfill our partner's needs; we are too needy ourselves. The partner who can forgo that fulfillment temporarily is an authentic ally—someone who, just by being present, helps us stabilize ourselves. We are now the Humpty-Dumpty who needs no king's horses or men, only the someone who loves us.

Even a partner who is also falling apart or not totally emotionally healthy can be of help. The friends of Dorothy on the road to Oz were not robust supermen—they were just limited, ragamuffin beings who needed her as much as she needed them. But they nonetheless stepped up as allies who helped her successfully. Even—maybe especially—it is the wounded folk who may help us more than we ever thought possible.

My own baby-boomer generation had many flaws, including in our parenting style. But from the not-so-good can come the better—eventually. We did start the self-help movement, which has had benefits for many who came after us. Indeed, sometimes we don't find out till later in life who helped us or how. "Helped us," by the way, is always the same as "still helping us," because we are still experiencing the benefits.

Spiritual Connection

Jung uses the phrase "friend of the soul" as a way of describing someone who communes with us at a deep level, the higher Self level. In chapter 2, we saw how the higher Self is this friend of the soul, our primary ally. In intimate partnership, an alive and loving alliance happens when one higher Self embraces another higher Self—two friends, one soul. Since the higher Self is the same in all of us, this makes perfect sense at a spiritual level too, the level at which all is one. We find this wisdom about relationships in the Bible too, for instance in the story of the friendship between the prince Jonathan and the future king, David: "The soul of Jonathan was knit to the soul of David and Jonathan loved him as his own soul" (1 Samuel 18:1). The reverse is the meeting of two egos—that is, the meeting of the flint and steel that makes the sparks fly up and the love fly away.

HOW TO GIVE FEEDBACK RATHER THAN CRITICISM

Feedback is essential to honest communication, and it can become an assisting force when we suggest a change that will make our relating more effective. But it's important to stay conscious of the difference between giving helpful feedback—the style of an ally—and being critical or judgmental of someone's choices or behavior—an afflicting experience. This distinction applies not only to relationships but also to interactions at work and elsewhere. Choosing to offer feedback rather than criticism is yet another way of practicing integrity and loving-kindness:

FEEDBACK (THE STYLE OF AN ALLY)	CRITICISM (THE STYLE OF A FAULTFINDER)
Is the style of an assisting force	Is the style of an afflicting force
Informs us	Shames us
Is supportive	Is blaming/scolding/impugning/attacking
Is a reasonable assessment or correction	Is a judgment against us or a condemnation
Is meant to help, improve, or encourage us	Is meant to show us how wrong or inadequate we are
Is motivated by caring about our progress and growth	Is motivated by censure, blaming, and disapproval
Has our best interests at heart	Has reproach or rebuke in mind
Maintains an equal playing field, seeking "win-win"	May be competitive, playing the ego game of "Gotcha!"
Can be all positive or include well-meant critiquing: constructive criticism	Is always negative
Is about how we can both benefit: "Let's explore together."	Is about who is right and who is wrong: "I know and you don't."
Always values and contributes to bonding	Is willing to or does break connection
Seeks to open a dialogue and to learn from each another	Closes down communication, is dismissive
Is given privately or with others present if both are okay with that	Might be private or might be in the presence of others, sometimes with the intent to embarrass us
Shows us by suggestion: a prompt	*Tells* us what is required: a poke
Feels trustworthy and inviting	Feels invasive or hurtful
Lifts us up	Puts us down

A fun practice is to teach our inner critic how to switch to the kindly style of feedback!

Both feedback and criticism can be hard-hitting; strong impact is sometimes a feature of being honest. However, when we practice loving-kindness and compassion, we are careful about how we present our feedback. We are straightforward but we do not want to hurt someone's feelings. In an intimate relationship, feedback is honest *and* kindly—the style of a genuinely assisting force. Ideally feedback comes in the form of an "I" statement, whereas criticism often is presented with a "you" statement.

Criticism: "You keep the volume on your radio too damn high and you obviously don't care how it affects other people."

Feedback: "I find loud music disturbing. It would help me if you could lower the volume."

When we are the recipients of feedback or criticism, we remain open rather than defensive or dismissive. We know we can learn something about ourselves from both feedback and criticism. In both, for instance, we find out how what we do impacts someone else, how we can be more effective in our relating, how we need to take a close look at our behavior or attitudes. We say "thanks" for feedback; we may, however, say "Ouch!" when we are criticized.

An aggressive person will blurt out a criticism without asking or caring if the other person is open to it or if the time is right for it. In contrast, before giving feedback a caring, respectful person asks if it is okay to do so, and if not, forgoes expressing it. A person in an overwhelmed state might not be ready for any suggestions or feedback for the time being. In loving-kindness, we want to honor that timing.

"A scoffer who is corrected will only hate you; the wise, when corrected, will love you," advises the Bible in Proverbs 9:8. We can't forget that someone with an excessively inflated ego will take even the most minor comments or feedback as an affront. That person interprets correction as criticism, hearing feedback as coming from the voice of his own inner critic. The big ego is thus disabled from receiving feedback. Such a fragile ego is afraid to be seen with all its vulnerabilities unfurled. Indeed, it is afraid to be thought of as lacking in even the slightest way. The stakes are even higher when the entitled, easily bruised ego is called out about its own narcissism. Then the sparks of rage and possibly retaliation can explode. These will not be sparks that kindle the campfire around which we can safely huddle and warmly bond. They will ignite the arson that burns down the cottage of conversation and closeness.

Closeness includes openness to feedback about how we impact each other, how we might trigger one another. Giving helpful feedback is part of the role of an assisting force. We welcome that ally energy when we listen without becoming defensive.

At the same time, we take care to be allies of our own selves, so we speak up if the feedback is blaming, inaccurate, or not useful.We may work out a mutually acceptable plan along these lines early in a relationship. Perhaps we say, "At any time, I welcome your feedback because it helps me. I want as much information as I can get about how I come across. So please feel free to call me out. I will stay open and not let my ego go on the defensive. But I will speak up, gently, if what you say about my behavior seems incorrect to me or judgmental. I will do this without becoming upset at you." This feedback arrangement won't work until partners have built at least some trust in one another. However, it will increase trust if they stay with it as a practice. (The phrase "stay with" is a reminder that our spiritual practices are indeed assisting forces!)

As a final consideration, we remind ourselves that if we were criticized, shamed, beaten in childhood we may reexperience trauma in any form of feedback that does not affirm us, however well-meant or truthful. Trauma leads to a trigger reaction that makes feedback threatening. Trauma can make questions from others about our choices come through as accusations, feedback sound like shaming, comments register as judgments. Our work is to admit our own trauma-induced woundedness to ourselves and those we want to relate to. We don't then ask for less feedback from others—only for more patience as we work through our trauma-driven reactions. Eventually, work on our triggers lets us hear feedback as kindly comment rather than accusation or shaming. This outcome is what makes our honest work on ourselves, so full of self-compassion, a wonderfully assisting force.

AFFIRMATION AS COMMITMENT

Affirmations are positive statements that are meant to activate our personal potential. By repeating them they gradually become true of us. The practice below offers a list of personal affirmations but with a new spin—we are stating them as our *commitments* to our partner. We will be declaring to our partner that we offer the love that respresents steadfast alliance. Indeed, love is only love when it includes a commitment to being an assisting force. Or conversely: the real identity of the assisting force is the forceful power of love, based on ties that go beyond vows or promises.

PRACTICE
AFFIRMATION AND COMMITMENT PRACTICE

To foster the love that lasts as a truly assisting force, we can exchange the following affirmations of our commitment to be assisting forces in one another's lives:

- You can count on me as your trustwothy ally.
- I live in contiuous solidarity with you.
- I love and care about you.
- I am always here as your go-to.
- I support your growth and evolution.
- I do all I can to foster your inner strengths.
- I attune to your feelings, needs, and longings.

- I can be trusted to be with you when you have to face or go through difficulties.
- I will help you stabilize when you feel you are breaking down.
- I am always available to pinch-hit for you until you can show up again.
- I look out for you.
- You can always turn to me.
- I am your friend.
- If you hurt me, I will say "Ouch!" but never retaliate.
- I can be trusted to come through for you.
- I encourage the best in you.
- I stand up for you.
- I am at your side.
- I offer you caring, committed connection.
- I show you attention, affection, appreciation, acceptance, allowing.
- I am committed to making the choices that deepen and enrich our relationship.
- I have ties to you that transcend time and distance.
- I am committed to being an assisting force in your life.
- I ask the same from you to whatever extent you can offer it.
- May my higher Self embrace your higher Self and yours mine.

May I show all the love I have in any way I can, today and all the time, to everyone, including myself, since love is what we are and why we're here. May all that happens to me be an opportunity of grace to love much more and fear much less. I dedicate myself to make this world one Sacred Heart of love.

5 SPIRITUAL, RELIGIOUS, AND MYTHIC ALLIES

May those who find themselves in a trackless and fearsome wilderness . . . be guarded by beneficent heavenly beings.

—Shantideva, *The Way of the Bodhisattva*

Shantideva's "trackless and fearsome wilderness" in *The Way of the Bodhisattva* describes viscerally what an isolated aloneness or exclusion feels like. Yet, he also references "beneficent heavenly beings" who come through as our allies and safeguard us from desolation.

The promise of assistance is a common archetypal thread in spiritual, religious, and mythic stories about a lonesome pilgrim.

The message is straightforward and encouraging: Any distress can be tolerated as long as we don't have to feel it alone, or endure without companionship in any severe helplessness, seclusion, or dogged fear. Any of us—and not by choice—can at times find ourselves loitering on the dark side of the moon. But it is terrifying to do that when we are alone. That is the equivalent of vanishing in the assembling mists, being lost in no-man's land, out of options, powerless indeed.

Since this predicament may be a given in any human life we can see why the Twenty-Third Psalm is so popular: "Yea, though I walk through the valley of the shadow . . . I will fear no evil for you are *with* me." I can "walk through" anything when there is a "with me." These words exemplify the power of a spiritual assisting or accompanying force that walks with us through the dark. The word "with" here is really both "with" and "within"—another example of the mystery of how spiritual assisting forces are with us and in us.

We can't understand a mystery but we can celebrate it. This happens when we begin to sense our wider identity, one that includes all our assisting forces. Walt Whitman perhaps had this in mind in his "Song of Myself": "I am large; I contain multitudes." Even without a belief in a divine shepherd, one can have a sense of an accompanying presence. In the familiar lyrics from *Carousel* by Oscar Hammerstein II, a heartful *hope* is the assisting force, without any specifically religious nomenclature:

When you walk through a storm . . .
Walk on . . .
With hope in your heart
And you'll never walk alone.

Thus, with or without faith, we can feel an invisible presence around us.

The song from *Carousel*, coincidentally, uses a phrase seen in the Twenty-Third Psalm: "walk through." In both the song and the psalm we feel ourselves accompanied by an assisting force as long as we keep going on. That fits with the way the archetype works: a journey will invite allies. The central archetype of a heroic journey always includes the archetype of assisting forces—a reason for hope.

Spiritual assisting forces can also, of course, become visible by faith. In one biblical story (Kings 6:15–17), the army of the Israelites seems small at first compared to that of their enemy as they go into battle, and a servant of the prophet Elisha asks, "Alas, master! What shall we do?" Elisha replies, "Do not be afraid, for there are more with us than there are with them." As the story continues, "The Lord opened the eyes of the servant, and he saw: the mountain was full of horses and chariots of fire all around Elisha."

The enlightened Indian Buddhist teacher Padmasambhava, says something similar: "I am never far away from those with faith, or even from those without it, *though they do not see me.* My children will always, always be protected by my compassion." Both of these passages offer the promise of "with-ness" on our journey. We also see another comforting quality of allies: we don't always have to seek them out; sometimes they come to us.

AWARENESS OF THE TRANSCENDENT

So far in this book we have used the words "more than" as a clue to the presence and meaning of the transcendent. The Victorian polymath John Ruskin wrote, "No human capacity ever yet saw the whole of a thing; but we may see more and more of it the longer we look." When a thing has become transcendent to us, as in the example of something we are drawn to in nature, it has become a reliable resource, even a refuge at times—hence an assisting force. Yet, it will take our looking longer and longer, as Ruskin advises, to appreciate its depths. When we look at ourselves in the mirror we don't see all that we are as humans. When we keep peering into the mystery dimension of ourselves we suddenly or gradually realize that we live in a higher Self, an identity that is more than our ego.

Likewise, an intense attentiveness to the natural world also reveals the more-than-meets-the-eye. We feel a sense of awe as we glimpse the divine in nature. Awe as our response to the "more" is the equivalent of adoration in a religious context. The fact that there is such an experience as awe suggests the presence of the transcendent, the divine in nature's pageant, aglow in the peacock's feathers, as the Romantic poet William Blake noticed: "The pride of the peacock *is* the glory of God."

The transcendent as the "more than" gives us a vastly expanded view of our existence:

- We see more in the world than only what meets the eye. We see a pulsing life force in the whole array of things. In the finite we catch a glimpse of something infinite.
- We see more in time than just duration. We see a portal into an eternal now, open to us in any and every moment.
- We see that there is more to us than just our ego identity. We are full of wisdom, love, and healing power in our higher Self— that is, we have Buddha nature, Christ consciousness, divine spirit, nature's life force within us.
- Spiritually and archetypally we see that there is more to us than our own individual bodymind. Our identity is far-reaching. It includes all our connections throughout our lifespan—especially our assisting forces, visible and invisible, human and nonhuman, mortal and immortal. They are all who we are now. Believing we are separate selves is nothing less than a case of mistaken identity.
- We embrace our present predicament and find more in it than a problem to be solved. It is a path to enlightenment, an assisting force contributing to our growth.
- We see more in our circumstances than just events. We see all that happens as opportunities for us to evolve into whole and wholesome humans.
- We grasp the fact that a feeling is more than its name, e.g., fear or anger. It includes a personally felt sense, an archetypal energy, a history unique to us, implications not even we can fully grasp.
- We see our work as more than a job or career. We feel a calling in it to cocreate a world of justice, peace, and love.
- We see love as more than a choice of what pleases us. It is an unconditionally caring, committed connection. We have a heart

that is more than a muscle—it is a sacred heart that can love infinitely and indefatigably.

- We see our circle of kinship as including more than our family and friends; we are members of the wider family and fellowship of earth, and we are indefatigably devoted to its care.
- We see something beyond what ordinary vision or thought can comprehend—a transcendent reality through, with, and in all that is.
- We see relating as more than a commitment to a partner. We feel our love expanding its scope so that our loving-kindness becomes universal in its reach.

The Buddhist idea of emptiness is ultimately about the more: there is an emptiness—that is, a lack of solid definition of things—and that means that there is an enormous spaciousness in them too. Meaningful things are more than meanings given in a dictionary. They are all dharma gates, openings into enlightenment. Using the analogy of a mirror on a wall, we can say that "empty" means open to all and anything. And thus anything can be an ally.

MYTHIC ALLIES

In ancient religion and myth, we often encounter the archetype of the assisting force. Vishnu, Christ, and Prometheus each represent the archetype of the gift-giving friend of humans. Incarnations and avatars are also examples of allies. "Incarnation" refers to the process by which a god takes human form. Such a person is referred to as "avatar" in Hindu tradition. In many myths and religious doctrines, gods take human form in order to help us.

An imaginative example of a supernatural assisting force is the genie—a magical spirit that can take many forms, as most allies do, in order to be of service to us. The genie in the bottle or from the magic lamp are colorful images of spirits with powers that go beyond the ordinary capacities of humans—the essence of an assisting force, the essence of spiritual assistance.

Spiritual seeking throughout the ages has included inquiry into the future with the aid of a shaman or the use of various divination techniques, such as consulting the I Ching, drawing cards from a tarot deck, or undertaking an astrology reading. Inasmuch as they may help us know ourselves in the moment and help us plan wisely for our future, these methods can be truly assisting forces in our lives.

Sometimes synchronicity—a meaningful coincidence, an unplanned moment that transcends cause and effect—may herald an opportunity in the present and perhaps for the future too. A synchronous experience can show us a new path, offer a new turn in a path, give a warning about the path we headed for, or serve as help on the path we are on. Synchronicity may even raise a cheer for how we have succeeded on the path. As an assisting force, synchronicity also announces to us when the time is "just right"—that is, just and right. In *The Accidental Universe*, the theoretical physicist Paul Davies proposes that "extraordinary physical coincidences and apparently accidental cooperation . . . offer compelling evidence that something is going on." He concludes, "A hidden principle seems to be at work, organizing the universe in a coherent way."

Synchronicities indicate, sometimes in an eerie way, that there is another realm beyond this one and that something in it wants to communicate directly with us. This element of communication is the equivalent of revelation in religion and corresponds to teachings and sutras in Buddhism. In claiming "A presence is never dumb," the French theologian Pierre Teilhard de Chardin was suggesting that the spiritual world *wants* to reach us. It tells its news in stories, divination, synchronicities, time, nature, all in us.

RELIGIOUS ALLIES

People in a religious community may find an assisting force in a priest, minister, rabbi, mullah, elder, or any guide or teacher. Part of many faiths is also believing in an invisible assisting force, a divine accompaniment. Universally, as people of faith look to an assisting force, many of the figures and rituals of religion stand as metaphors for energies in the collective archetype of that force. The wise Zen master is certainly a personification of the wise old man or woman, an archetype of the collective unconscious. In the traditional theistic viewfinder, God is the central ally of humanity (as with the worshiper in Psalm 119:24, who sings to the Lord: "Your statutes are my delight, they are my counselors"). Enduring faith in God as guide and defender is most powerful when it is based on an *experience* of this divine accompanying presence—an experience that can happen either all at once in special moments or in an ongoing way.

In the faith story, companionship is important not only toward us from God (or from *a* god) but also from us toward that god. Indeed, in the *Bhagavad Gita*, the god Krishna creates so that *he can have* companions.

In the Christian understanding, companionship with God comes through Jesus, who commits himself to be the eternal ally of humanity: "Behold, I am with you always," he says in Matthew 28:20. "I will not leave you comfortless; I will come to you," he promises in John 14:18. He also sends an *advocate*, his Holy Spirit: "I will ask the father and he will send you another advocate to be with you always." St. Paul writes of this advocate: "The Spirit helps us in our weakness" (Romans: 8: 26).

The divine feminine is also significant in spiritual advocacy. St. John Chrysostom, in a hymn to Mary, an example of the divine feminine, commemorating her leaving earth for heaven, says, "You went away but you never left us." This realization implies belief in an enduring presence even during a physical absence.

The religious assisting forces, especially the guides, remind us that our ego does not have sufficient gear for a fully successful spiritual journey. Heroes and heroines in myths, for instance, were not able to explore the underworld, the unconscious, without a spiritual guide or special amulet. But there is another angle to this: mythic characters needed a divine assisting force for another reason. It was to save themselves from *hubris*, the arrogant illusion that humans don't need assistance from any power higher than ego. Thus these types of guides are more than companions into the dark—they protect our souls from falling into the pit of ego grandiosity.

GUARDIAN ANGELS

Another figure that represents the assisting force is the guardian angel, depicted as a companion, guide, and protector. Angels are personifications of the archetype of the assisting force. Shakespeare's Hamlet, in his fear during act 3 of the story, cries for an angelic ally and protector: "Save me, and hover o'er me with your wings / You heavenly guards!" (In act 1 he had pleaded, "Angels and ministers of grace defend us!") The presence of an individual guardian angel at our side is a common belief in ancient religions and in the Judeo-Christian tradition. Ruins of an Assyrian palace, now in the British Museum, show an image of such a guardian spirit about whom Nabopolasser, the father of Nebuchadnezzar, inscribed, "The god Marduk sent a tutelary angel of grace to be at my side. In everything I undertook he brought me success." Plato in *The Phaedo* has Socrates comment, just before his death, "When the dead arrive at the place to which each has been led by his own guardian spirit . . ."

In the Hebrew Bible, God says to Moses, "My angel shall go before you" (Genesis 32:34). Likewise, in the book of Tobias, Raphael, the angel of healing, guards Tobias. Psalm 90:11 says: "He has given his angels charge over you; to keep you [safe] in all your ways." In chapter 10 of the book of Daniel, individual angels are assigned as protectors over each district of the city.

The New Testament includes many instances of angelic presences: St. Joseph has an ally in the angel who warns him to flee to Egypt to protect the endangered newborn Jesus. As an adult, Jesus says, speaking of children, "Their angels in heaven always see the face of my Father in heaven" (Matthew 18:10). An angel comes to comfort Jesus in his agony in the garden of Gethsemane just prior to his arrest, and later an angel frees St. Peter from prison. Hebrews 1:14 adds, "Are not all angels ministering spirits sent to serve those who will inherit salvation?" In every appearance of these angels as guardians and helpers in the Judeo-Christian texts, we recognize the qualities of the ally archetype. Later Christian writers proposed that an angel is assigned to everyone. For instance, St. Thomas Aquinas stated that "not only baptized people but every soul that comes into this world receives a guardian spirit." Aquinas wrote that these guardians even stay with us after we die and join us in heaven "to enlighten us"—a quality of allies. Likewise, St. Jerome, in "Commentary on Matthew," saw the guardian angel archetype as universal: "How great the dignity of the human soul, since each one has from birth an angel commissioned to guard it."

Recall that whatever an archetype offers to us is always a calling to us: we are deputized by spiritual assisting forces to do for others what they do for us. This relay makes sense and is quite doable since an archetype represents an intrinsic capacity and inclination in every human. Thus, in *The Tao of Liberation*, the authors Mark Hathaway and Leonardo Boff encourage us: "We can choose to be guardian angels who protect, care for, and transform the earth into a common home for all, the entire earthly and cosmic community." Truly loyal companions have been known to sacrifice anything, everything, for what or those we hold dear.

Reminiscent of the idea of a guardian spirit accompanying each person, no matter how unworthy we seem to be or how far away we stray, we hear the Soto Zen master Dogen say, "All Buddhas of the past, present, and future are practicing together with each person." We note he says "each person," not "only the enlightened persons." An ally will come to us when we have hope in our heart, as the song says. Hope invites allies.

FINDING THE SOUL'S ALLY

We have seen how our higher Self is our primary ally. Now we deepen our understanding and look at how wide the spiritual range of that higher Self may be. We begin with a passage from Carl Jung's *Psychology and Alchemy*:

> The "treasure hard to attain" [another name for the philosopher's stone, the goal of alchemy] lies hidden in the ocean of the unconscious, and only the brave can reach it. I conjecture that the treasure is also the "companion," the one who goes through life at our side—in all probability a close analogy to the lonely ego who finds a mate in the Self. . . . This is the theme of the magical, traveling companion.

This "companion" is the invisible partner who is at the same time ourselves—in other words, a spiritual twin, like a guardian angel. The yearning for such a companion is, of course, in all of us humans. Jung describes the outcome of discovering that companion:

> It is the state of someone who, in his wanderings among the mazes of his psychic transformation, comes upon a secret happiness which reconciles him to his apparent loneliness. In communing with himself, he finds not deadly boredom and melancholy but an inner partner; more than that, a relationship that seems like the happiness of a secret love, or

like a hidden springtime. . . . It is the alchemical *benedicta viriditas*, the blessed greenness."

SPIRITUAL FRIENDSHIP

Religious people over the centuries have often referred to spiritual companionship and assistance as relationship to a "spiritual friend." The Gaelic word *anamchara* translates as "soul-friend." In the *Martyrology of Oengus*, St. Brigid of Kildare is given these words: "Anyone without a soul-friend is like a body without a head." As an assisting force on our journey, the soul-friend is the reliable confidant with whom we can share our innermost spiritual conundrums, visions, and realizations.

In a work titled *Spiritual Friendship*, St. Aelred (1111–1167), the Cistercian abbot of Rievaulx Abbey in medieval England, expands on Cicero's essay "On Friendship"—celebrating trust and affection between friends who cherish one another's presence in their lives. St. Aelred's work was also influenced by St. Augustine, who said he found "the greatest delight in companions." Aelred's words remind us of the elements of joy and love that arise in us when we feel the presence of an ally who wants only our best good, and they reflect the idea that spiritual friends are assisting forces because they are contributors to one another's spiritual practice and progress:

> It is no small consolation in this life to have someone who can unite with you in an intimate affection and the embrace of a holy love. Someone in whom your spirit can rest, to whom you can pour out your soul, to whose pleasant exchanges, as to soothing songs, you can fly in sorrow. To the dear breast of whose friendship, amidst the many troubles of the world, you can safely retire. A person who can shed tears with you in your worries, be happy with you when things go well, search out with you the answers to your

problems, whom with the ties of charity you can lead into the depths of your heart. A person who, though absent in body, is yet present in spirit, where heart to heart you can talk to him, where the sweetness of the Spirit flows between you, where you so join yourself and cleave to him that soul mingles with soul and two become one.

In Buddhism we find the idea of *kalyana-mittata*, "virtuous friendship," in which spiritual friends support one another's practice with candidness, wisdom, and trustworthiness. In the *Upaddha Sutra*, Buddha explained to Ananda—his disciple, cousin, and friend—that such spiritual companionship can be considered the whole of the Dharma as the "holy life." Buddha went on to say that when we have *kalyana-mittata* in place with friends, they cheer and encourage us on the path—and when our friend is Buddha, we are fully freed from suffering. In the *Dighajanu Sutra*, Buddha says that when a practitioner is committed to dialogue with a variety of upstanding people, he learns to imitate their commitment to the Dharma, their compassion, their discerning wisdom. They have become allies of enlightenment to one another.

Another text, the *Anguttara Nikaya*, lists the qualities of a monastic spiritual friend: he is amiable, venerable, able to give good counsel, patient in listening, respectful, capable of speaking in depth about the Dharma, and serious enough to share on a depth level. A helpful teacher is a prime example of a spiritual friend when she offers guidance, challenges, comfort, and cheer—all the scaffolding of authentic support.

A support group, a faith community, or a local sangha are examples of groups of spiritual friends.

Peer companionship is certainly valuable on the spiritual path. Our spiritual practice and our psychological health are enlivened when we have a trusted friend to whom we can speak openly about ourselves. This spiritual ally will not be the "friend" who flatters and inflates our ego—a narcissistic style of alliance. The ally of our higher Self supports our journey toward generosity, humility, enlightenment, and loving-kindness. This ally warns and saves us from what in Buddhism are called the three poisons: greed, hate, and ignorance—that is, the illusion of separateness. These poisons are descriptors of the inflated ego at its worst. Spiritual friends will be the ones who show and lead us from greed to generosity, from hate to love, and from ignorance to wisdom.

Ubuntu is an African term meaning "humanity toward others." It is also translated as "I am because you are" or "I am what I am because of who we all are." The ubuntu philosophy tells us that all beings can be allies, contributing to our becoming what we can best be in this moment. Ubuntu is also a spiritual calling to reach out to and care about all beings as relatives in the family of humanity. Ubuntu transcends race and creed. All diversity becomes, or rather is, only one reality—just what the Buddhas and mystics in all traditions came to realize. We feel an intense, ineradicable sense of belonging and we pass on to others that same joyous sense. We remind ourselves that we are not stand-alone beings; we exist only *with* everyone else, the solidarity that Thich Nhat Hanh calls "inter-being."

We can observe unanimous agreement among the assisting-counseling forces in all times and traditions: we can only be allies to one another if there are no boundaries to our assisting outreach. Indeed, such boundaries are really barriers. The wise, courageous, assisting forces in all traditions have made the journey from insulation to universal embrace. They see diversity as a path to unity. Their caring, committed connection has no frontier. There will always be differences among us, but none that have to make a difference.

As our sense of being surrounded by assisting forces we come to trust these words of the poet Christopher Smart: "We never are deserted quite."

6 THE TRICKSTER WHO AFFLICTS AND ASSISTS

The figure of the trickster is a forerunner of the savior and like him, both god, man, and animal all at once. He is both sub-human and superhuman, bestial and divine. His chief and most alarming characteristic is his unconsciousness. The so-called civilized man has forgotten the trickster. He remembers him only figuratively and metaphorically, when, irritated by his own ineptitude, he speaks of fate playing tricks on him or of things being bewitched. He never suspects that his own hidden and apparently harmless shadow has qualities that are exceedingly dangerous.

—Carl Jung, *Archetypes and the Collective Unconscious*

Let's begin with a look at the dictionary definition of the word "trickster": a dishonest person who defrauds others by trickery, who practices crafty underhanded stratagems to deceive or cheat. The trickster is thus a deceptive character who dupes us with cunning ingenuity for his own gain or profit. He is the master of hoax. The trickster archetype, however, has other qualities and purposes. He deceives us for our own gain! At first, the trickster may appear to be only an afflicting force, but finally we may recognize him as an assisting force too.

The trickster is the devious character we meet in the folklore of many cultures, who, humorously or not, turns the world upside down. The trickster appears as the snake oil salesman, the con artist, the impostor, the clown, the charlatan, the swindler, the joker, the prankster who may hurt us but also will teach us, through hard knocks, about our own limits and self-deception. When he shows up in our own life, the trickster topples, fools, or hoodwinks us to show us how vulnerable we are, how flimsy is our self-proclaimed grandiosity, how gullible we can be, how easily we can be deceived no matter how high our IQ.

The trickster character in stories and myths is elfishly mischievous, greedy, selfish. He tricks people and yet often helps, heals, or saves them. Some examples of the animal versions of the trickster are the coyote among the Native Americans, the spider in African folklore, the monkey in China. Loki, the Norse trickster god, is a shape-shifter, easily changing his gender or his looks, even becoming an animal or fish when that serves his purpose: to deceive us into higher consciousness. Satan, the devil, is a trickster in Abrahamic religious traditions. Hermes is the trickster in Greek myth, to whom Homer says in *The Iliad*: "Hermes, you exceed the other gods because you are our companion." The trickster archetype—like all the archetypes—can in fact be both an afflicting force and an assisting force. In cartoons, the trickster meets us as the Road Runner, not only to trip us up but also to show us our ego's wiles are not successful—though humility will be. Since the first step on the spiritual path is letting go of ego, this is an example of how what afflicts us can assist us.

We might fear danger from the shadow figure or trickster who's trying to break into our cozy world, but scarier than that is the trickster inside ourselves. Every one of us can meet up with the trickster or become him to ourselves or others. The quotation from Jung at the beginning of this chapter reminds us that the greatest danger is in not recognizing this trickster energy in ourselves or in the people who aim it at us. An archetype is often a hidden force or impetus behind our decisions. It is therefore crucial to keep its energy conscious. Then we relate to it. When an archetype remains unconscious, it can possess us, rule us, control us, harm us and others. These negative reactions happen because we are denying, masking, or keeping unconscious the very traits in ourselves that we fear or hate in others. We will then keep projecting the energy of that archetype instead of acknowledging what Emily Dickinson calls "our self behind our self concealed."

When we acknowledge a projected energy in ourselves, no matter how unwelcome or disturbing, we are free—that is, no longer compelled to enact what we have so long kept hidden from ourselves. Ironically, we ultimately come to know ourselves by letting go of all our ways of being sure we won't know ourselves.

The trickster as an archetype is a feature of human nature, inherited from our ancient past, that has become a natural inclination—like an instinct in an animal. In chapter 1 we explored one kind of archetype that appears over and over in history, as a character in stories or in our life story. In subsequent chapters we explored another kind of archetype: a spiritual *event*, especially an initiatory event in life or in stories, mythic or religious. Examples of these archetypal events are death and rebirth, ascension, resurrection, transfiguration, initiation, incarnation, grace. Religion over the centuries preserves in its beliefs and rituals a treasury of both these varieties of archetypal energy. Examples of characters are gods and saints. Examples of events are what those characters do or make happen, miracles included. The trickster is an archetype that combines character and event. Thus the trickster energy that traumatically deceived us (character archetype) may turn out to be the one that fostered our initiation (transformative event archetype)—an afflicting force becomes an assisting force.

The trickster usually exhibits a comic element. Humor thrives on contrast, oxymoron. The trickster loves turning everything topsy-turvy. Listening to the news on CNN, we hear serious reporting of daily occurrences. It comes through to us as new information.

Listening to Stephen Colbert or Bill Maher, we hear comedic versions of news events. They say what we already knew but might have been afraid to say publicly. They also poke fun at accepted norms. In other words, they are the helpful tricksters so necessary in a society. They are like the king's fool in medieval times, allowed to point to the errors in authority without penalty. Without those voices we are lost in a penal colony, subjected to diversity-killing totalitarianism.

Cartoon characters are contemporary personifications of the trickster. They too relish the disruption of the status quo, turning the ordered world into a dizzying abyss, everything becoming inchoate and chaotic but in the end restored to order and sanity. Although the characters themselves may not change, their world and its inhabitants—including ourselves—are transformed by their amusing antics. In fact, the trickster uses laughter to make characters see the absurdity of their lack of ego control and thereby perhaps force a change in the status quo, either in society or in us. There is a power in our own laughter at the human comedy that can help us change—that is, can help us move from being ruled by our own controlling ego to letting go of its fear-based control so something altogether new can emerge.

The trickster directly reshapes the world in three stages: first comes an upset of an antiquated order, followed by extreme disorder, and then a new, more expansive order is established. The trickster shows us the positive power of the disorder our ego has feared for too long. (Fear itself is also our best reminder that we still have an ego!) When ego bows to the trickster arsonist, Buddha appears in an all-enlightening flash.

In some faith traditions, we might also meet up with negative trickster energy in a realm beyond the human: "For our struggle is not against flesh and blood," wrote St. Paul about this invisible and ominous power, but rather it is "against the powers of this dark world and against the spiritual forces of evil in the heavenly realms" (Ephesians 6:12). As with all the archetypes, the trickster energy can transcend persons and exist, usually elusively, somehow in the atmosphere around us. In this form it is hard to see it, let alone integrate it. As such, we will have to turn to our spiritual assisting forces for help.

TRICKING THE COLLECTIVE

Thomas Paine's *Common Sense* declared, "The purpose of government is to protect society"—laws and leaders exist to support the rights of all of us. Government as an assisting force to society is the worthwhile mission of a democratic system. Its true executive leader leads with heart, not guns. Collective trickster energy, however, can produce what looks like a leader, a societal assisting force, though that person is really an afflicting force—for instance a leader who is ultimately, by wish or fact, a fascist or autocrat. This person is the showman, the Pied Piper who comes along over and over in history. He is a trickster who is able to persuade a consequential portion of a nation's population to follow his lead. He does this by pandering to the basest elements of the human shadow: greed, hate, and ignorance—the three poisons of enlightened living. The trickster leader assures his supporters that he will enact a policy of inequitable greed all in their favor, hateful division so as to activate their aggression, and ignorance or denial of the truth to boost and confirm their paranoia.

- He makes promises, but he doesn't deliver.
- He tells and spreads lies, "fake news."
- He promises that the nation under his leadership will be the greatest of all countries—a peace-endangering ego wish—but actually he lowers his country's status among the nations.
- He promises law and order, but actually he brings lawlessness and havoc.

- He promises prosperity for all, but actually he brings riches to himself and his donors rather than to those who need assistance.
- He promises unity, but he creates division.
- He blames undeserving scapegoats to distract the nation's population from his own woeful inadequacy.
- He attracts the uneducated and the excluded and can goad them into violence.
- He promises democracy, but he moves toward authoritarianism.
- He promises that he will keep borders safe from entry by those who are already disparaged by society.
- He focuses blame for societal ills on the people who are already looked down upon.
- He promises a wall to protect the nation, but he puts up walls everywhere between the citizens of that nation.

After a political trickster's downfall or loss of power, there will be collective post-traumatic stress both among those who supported him and among those who did not support him. This post-traumatic stress can best be healed by a collective grief process and a collective enthusiasm for the rebuilding of society. It will include a restoration of democratic ideals. Yet after the downfall there may instead be civil division, violence, insurrection, and increasingly blind beliefs in conspiracy theories.

The fact that this type of trickster keeps appearing in history shows that trickster energy is somehow appealing, sometimes even to the majority. Supporters of freedom and democracy will definitely have to keep an eye out if they are not to be conned by collective trickster energy. The bullying trickster shows us all how fragile both freedom and democracy are. Jung comments in book 9 of his *Collected Works*: "If a trick is successful, there is immediately created . . . that world of primordial darkness where everything that is characteristic of the trickster can happen, even on the highest plane of civilization." In other words, a society is prey to trickster energy no matter how civilized it imagines itself to be.

There is an irony in the dictatorial Pied Piper character: the autocrat who demands others follow his dictates ultimately *opposes* genuine trickster energy. The genuine, creative trickster is an assisting force who takes a stand against established norms and prevailing beliefs. He represents the healthy inclination to go beyond strictures, censures, constraints, unexamined norms, and antiquated rules: "Without deviation from the norm progress is not possible," Frank Zappa once commented. The helpful trickster laughs at reprimands, because his main purpose is to break through the limitations and injunctions people have unwittingly bought into from society and religion. This trickster invites us to be eccentric, marginal, not mainstream. He thereby opens us to creative alternatives.

The dictatorial trickster does the opposite. He prohibits creative alternatives. In addition, he lacks the subtlety it takes to move a population toward unity and wide-angle perspectives. So even as a personification of the trickster archetype, such a Piper is nothing but "the great pretender."

A SURPRISING REVERSAL

We have heard the warning that "pride goes before the fall." There is indeed something about the hubris in any of us that forecasts a fall. Hubris is the arrogant pride that denies it needs help from, or has been helped by, an assisting force. The trickster is the person who comes along in our life and shows us how wrong we are to be like that. The trickster gives our arrogant ego the comeuppance it fears but needs. The fall will be excruciating while it is happening, but ultimately it helps us. In relationships, the trickster who gives us a comeuppance is the two-timer who fools or betrays us or the charmer who ghosts us when we were so sure our bond would be enduring. These are instances of reversals of whatever we expected when we were overly prideful about ourselves.

Trickster energy appears in any event that has turned our life upside down and showed us how fragile we really are. A handsome face carries trickster energy if we believed it would bring us lasting happiness. Alcohol and drugs are the trickster when we become addicted to them; they promised escape but made us prisoners. Sexual desire can certainly be a trickster when it leads us astray from our life goals—for instance when infidelity destroys our cherished connections. In every such instance, trickster energy will absorb our focus, misdirect our choice, fool us into making mistakes, seduce us into believing we will achieve an increase of personal stature at no cost. In fact, the trickster is making the same promises to us that the serpent made to Eve—and we know how that story turned out.

Trickster energy can also work as a *positive spiritual reversal* of what we expect, as when the downtrodden powerless overcome their oppressors—lowly persons who overcome the so-called great, seemingly invulnerable person are the best sort of trickster comeuppance. The story of poor peasants who conquer rich nobles and dethrone Prince John, thanks to the trickster mischief of Robin Hood and his outlaw band of Merry Men of Sherwood, is one example of trickster legend in which marginal people are ultimately victorious over a strong force. In history, a similar outcome was achieved by Christian martyrs over the Roman empire.

In biblical references, the trickster appears subtly as a divine assisting force that reverses everything in favor of a new order, breaking the ego's tenuous hold on human enterprises. The powers that be become the powers that have been. For instance Mary sings a hymn in Luke 1:52–53: "He has pulled down the mighty from their thrones. He has exalted the lowly. He has filled the hungry with good things and sent the rich away empty." And Mary's hymn is itself based on 1 Samuel 2:7–8 in the Hebrew Bible, in which Hannah, mother of Samuel, sings, "The Lord . . . raises the poor from the dust and lifts the needy from the ash heap; he seats them with princes and has them inherit a throne of honor."

We see the same theme of reversal in this passage from St. Paul (1 Corinthians 1:26–28):

> Brothers and sisters think of what you were when you were called. Not many of you were wise by human standards, not many were influential, not many were of noble birth, but God chose the foolish things of the world to shame the wise. God chose the weak things of the world to shame the strong. God chose the lowly things of this world and the despised things, even the things that are not to nullify the things that are.

Such reversals of order also occur in the Buddhist tradition, as with the lowly Hui Neng—a simple layman with no formal education—who understands the Dharma better than any of the formal teachers. He becomes their patriarch and a teacher who is still helping humanity.

That kind of perfect trickster-style reversal is also a cause of hope, because we realize we don't have to be wise, we don't have to be influential, we don't have to be above everybody else to make a contribution to humanity. There's something in the higher Self we share in that can be of service to the universe, even though each of us may have little to offer by human standards.

Along the same lines, someone who becomes a whistleblower or stands up alone against a big corporation, against society itself, or even against a bully, shows a trust in assisting forces. That person is trusting the power of inner perseverance to enlist powers of support. Andrew Jackson famously said, "One person with courage is a majority."

Aesop's charming fable about the lion and the mouse is a time-honored example of how a lowly character helps a great character. The lion catches the mouse, who bargains for his life—promising that someday he will help the lion in return for his freedom. The lion laughs, saying he is the king of the jungle and would never need help from a paltry little mouse. Nonetheless, he releases the mouse—and later, when the lion is trapped in a net by human hunters, the mouse shows up in time to gnaw the ropes of the net and set the lion free. The mouse as savior is a great reversal indeed. We notice in the mouse's role two now-familiar elements of the assisting force: he promises presence and he comes through without having been asked. The mouse also helped the king of the jungle become more humble after all. We know we are truly humble when we are no longer ashamed of being humbled.

Cartoons offer many examples of the small character deflating the ego of the pompous character: The little mouse Jerry continually overcomes the big cat, Tom. Wile E. Coyote is a canine, much higher in the biological chain than a bird, yet over and over again he is defeated by the Road Runner. Br'er Rabbit, a recurring character in African American folktales, uses his wits to outsmart the predatory Br'er Fox. Bugs Bunny continually evades his tormentors through his hijinks and chicanery—the rascally rabbit perfectly exemplifies the clever nature of the trickster. Bugs's adversaries Elmer Fudd and Yosemite Sam are both human, yet Bugs wins every time.

(I once spoke to a woman who wrote children's books and she told me the most successful ones were those in which the child character somehow knows more than the adults or saves the day when the adults cannot. See how the archetype of the trickster was certainly known to us—and appreciated—from early on in life?)

The trickster energy in the cartoon stories, however, is not about how one character—for example, the Road Runner—always wins and another—such as Wile E. Coyote—always loses. The deeper meaning is that the win-lose style altogether misses the point. The characters' interactions invite us to let go of those rigidly competitive categories in favor of an inclusive alternative. We move from "How can I win?" to "How can we all have fun?" The Dodo in *Alice in Wonderland* comes pretty close to this exquisite wisdom when he proclaims, "Everybody has won and all must have prizes."

ALICE SHOWS US

The character of Alice in *Alice's Adventures in Wonderland* gives us a prime example of how trickster energy moves us into higher consciousness. Alice follows the White Rabbit down a hole into the depths of the earth—in other words, down into her own inner life, into her own unconscious, the hidden world. One of the skills of a trickster is that he can bring us into our own inner darkness and there we find out that we are bigger than we thought we were or smaller than we think we are. That descent into darkness is how Alice discovered the hitherto unknown reaches of her surprising unknown self. We can ask ourselves, "Who has been the White Rabbit in my life? How far into myself would I be willing to go to follow the trickster? Who is the trickster in my life today? And "Do I dare sing, 'Hello darkness, my old *friend*'?"

Sometimes in life we are at the helm; sometimes we are only passengers—or even stowaways—when the great voyage begins. The story of Alice in Wonderland reminds us that the heroic journey does not have to be one engineered by us. It can happen *to* us. Although, for instance, the knight Sir Galahad heroically takes the lead in the quest for the Holy Grail, Alice is *led* into her journey by another presence—as in her conversation with the trickster Cheshire cat.

When Alice asks the Cheshire cat, "Would you tell me please which way I ought to go from here?" the cat replies, "That depends a good deal on where you want to get to." "I don't much care where," says Alice. "Then it doesn't matter which way you go," said the cat. "As long as I get somewhere," Alice adds as an explanation. "Oh, you're sure to do that," says the cat, "if you only walk long enough."

In this little conversation, the trickster cat gives enigmatic and wily answers, but ultimately he's helping Alice because he's recommending following one's nose on the human journey. The assisting force turns us back to ourselves for the guidance we seek outside ourselves: the Cheshire cat reminds Alice that she doesn't have to turn to an authority to find out how to go or where to go.

We all have that wisdom in ourselves—a great reversal of how the world imagines things to be. All we have to do is walk. In other words, as long as we keep going, even in dread of the dark, we will feel accompanied by an assisting force—our interior courage, the ally walking beside or within us. Indeed, the demon of fear itself can become less threatening when we host it rather than attempt to evict it. Then fear no longer trips us; it only accompanies us while we walk through the valley of the shadow.

The trickster characters galore in Wonderland trick Alice into higher consciousness. We do not have to fear that the worst will foreclose on the better if we work with this kind of energy. The best can result. For example, we are fired from a job and then we find a better one—or a whole new and more suitable career. At first it looks like we lost everything. But then it turns out we found something much bigger and better. Indeed, we became bigger and better.

We might now ask ourselves questions like these: How has such a reversal happened to us in the course of our lives? How can we be on the lookout for it from now on? How can we build our trust that reversals have transformative power, one way or another? "The same old demons will always come up until finally you have learned your lesson, the lesson they came to teach you. Then those same demons will appear as friendly, warmhearted companions on the path," the Buddhist teacher Pema Chödrön advises in *The Wisdom of No Escape.*

7 THOSE WHO HAVE PASSED

After death our spirits shall be led
To those that love eternally.
                                 —Shakespeare, *The Two Noble Kinsmen*

In recent months, I watched two interviews about Judy Garland. One was with her costar Mickey Rooney. The other was with her daughter, Liza Minelli. In both interviews I heard how they felt, in a very real way, that Judy Garland was somehow still with them, that they could turn to her—*did* turn to her—for help in hard times. I do this with my own long-dead but cherished relatives. In my heart I ask them for help or accompaniment from time to time. I have come to trust that they hear me in some way, no proof required or expected.

One might call this poppycock or superstition. No one ultimately knows for sure about the fate of those who preceded us. But a natural faith leads many of us to believe our departed, smile-alight grandmas still care about us in some mysterious way—no need on our part to know for sure. And yes, we might also wonder if this is our tricky way of cheating death of his scythe? Or are we seeing how death too can relent? (I, for one, need and welcome all the comfort I can get, whether or not verifiable.)

In a way, the presence of friends or relatives *as their presence now exists in us* is actually the same whether they are alive or dead. "All I had to do was look at the palm of my hand, feel the breeze on my face, or the earth under my feet to remember that my mother is always with me, available at any time," Thich Nhat Hanh writes in *No Death, No Fear*. Years back, Father Al Giaquinto was my mentor and model of compassion and spiritual insight. He spent his last years in Baltimore while I lived in California. I knew I would never see him again. When I heard that he had died I was sad. But I also understood that he was in my consciousness in the same way as when he was alive. Since he existed only at a distance anyway, the *kind* of distance did not matter. Father Al was three thousand miles away for so many years. Now he is an eternity away but the absence or presence is ultimately the same. He is as absent now as he was before and as present now as he will ever be. So how can death interfere with how I still benefit from his help—and sense of an assisting presence in my life? I am now recalling St. John Chrysostom: "Those whom we love and lose are no longer where they were before; they are now wherever we are."

In a related context, a worker for equality will be comforted by the memory of Martin Luther King Jr.'s idealism and courage and receive what feels like support directly from King though he is physically gone. In addition to support in our acts of fortitude, when we lose faith in our calling and become discouraged, it can be the fervor of saintly others, alive or dead, that keeps us afloat.

Since so many separations in daily life have led to reconnections, it is no wonder that so many people come to believe that death, the ultimate separation, will lead to reconnection. Many traditions hold that we go on after death or that communication with those who have died is possible. In Tibetan Buddhism, for instance, the soul of the person who died passes through bardos, intermediate stages between death and the next life. In these states the soul is aided by bodhisattvas, spiritual assisting forces.

In Christianity there is a sacrament called Holy Communion. It entails a pledge to be allies to all humanity—that is, to be committed to love for all people, free of all divisiveness and bias. Likewise, there is a belief in a "communion of saints." The saints are those who have lived out the communion pledge and, upon death, become assisting forces to us who are still alive here on earth. They are helping us from the other side of the grave, and we can ask for their help from this side. Thus the doctrine of communion of saints proclaims that the archetype of the assisting force is enduring—that is, triumphant over death. In the posthumous 1964 volume *Markings*, the secretary-general of the United Nations Dag Hammarskjöld refers to this teaching: "Through me there flashes this vision of a magnetic field in the soul, created in a timeless present by unknown multitudes . . . whose words and actions are a timeless prayer. 'The Communion of Saints'—and—within it—an eternal life." According to St. Thomas Aquinas, the communion of saints includes all people—not just those who are or were religious. Aquinas acknowledges, as Buddhism does, that there is an indissoluble link among all beings whether alive or dead, practitioners or not. Rumi wrote, "There is a community of the spirit . . . flowing down and down in ever-widening rings of being."

In the communion of saints doctrine, those in heaven are called "saints." A "patron saint" refers to an ally or protector archetype with a specific focus. For instance, in Catholicism, each country has its own patron saint. Believers also may turn to certain saints because they are associated with specific concerns about which they can be of help. So for instance, St. Francis is the patron of animals and there is a special blessing of animals given annually on his commemorative day, October 4. Believers can pray to him for the well-being of their pets. St. Lucy is the patron saint of the eyes. Hence people pray to her when they have eye disease. The concept of a patron saint can also include a back-and-forth style of accompaniment: people with faith can believe that when they have an eye problem, St. Lucy is already coming to their aid without their having to ask. In the communion of saints teaching, all the saints are praying and looking out for all of us. The archetype of the assisting force looks for us rather than waits for us. The guardian comes to us even unbidden. We recall the Beatles song about how in troublesome times we can trust a mother energy, using the name Mary, to show up with wise words for us though we did not ask.

Like all the archetypes, the assisting force thus includes the element of outreach. It is always trying to come through for us, even seeking us out. In Ezekiel 34:11, God says: "Behold, I myself will search for my sheep and seek them out." In this passage, and in the concept of a patron saint or bodhisattva, we see that the assisting force does what love does—reaches out on its own. All assisting and accompanying forces are thus practicing loving-kindness toward us and all beings. Here is a fascinating example from nature showing how assisting forces come unbidden to where they are needed: every year winds deliver millions of tons of phosphorous- and iron-rich sand from the Sahara Desert all the way across the Atlantic Ocean, carrying nutrients to the Amazon, which is so in need of them.

As we keep aging we see our friends and family members passing away one by one. We grieve because the duke of death is depopulating our circle of loving companions so inexorably, so ruthlessly. More and more we have to rely on ourselves and our dwindling sources of comradeship. As this happens we may notice an increase in our trust in help from the lost ones too. This tendency fits with belief in the communion of saints, because those who loved us are saints to us indeed—and in deed.

TURNING TO THE ANCESTORS

Belief in the spiritual presence of ancestral assisting forces is perennial in the human psyche. For instance, in ancient Roman times people venerated the "Lares," or spirits of the ancestors. We see this honoring of ancestors in Asian religion too. The saints and bodhisattvas are spiritual ancestors. From this we might infer that our contemporary helpers are not sufficient as sources of nurturance and alliance; we also need help from earlier generations. Or, another way of saying it: we need all the help we can get.

In ancient Greek religion we see a reference to those who passed away yet now are helping us: "According to Hesiod, the souls delivered from birth are at rest and absolved. They become guardian spirits of humankind. . . . Like old athletes, they do not lose interest in us but show goodwill and sympathetic zeal toward us still engaged in life, setting forth with us and shouting encouragement as they see us approach, and at last attain, our hoped-for goal," notes the philosopher Plutarch in *De genio Socratis* 24. Cecil Maurice Bowra, in his book *Pindar,* says the dead listen to the poetry of that Greek lyric poet: "Deep in the earth their heart listens." Since poetry is certainly something to turn to in distress, we see how it too is an assisting force beyond the limits of time.

Ancestors can also, on the other hand, represent and bequeath epigenetic trauma—that is, trauma passed down to us from their life experience long ago. An example is a history of pogroms culminating in the Holocaust. We might carry the scars of those atrocities visited upon our ancestors. Our trauma work is then not only personal but also ancestral. Our ancestors may be able, in some mysterious way, to help us also in the working through of trauma. It will be up to us to call upon them to do so. It's worth a try. The healing process may also happen in reverse: When we heal ourselves of epigenetic trauma, we heal our ancestors too. The result may be that future generations do not suffer as our ancestors did and as we do.

We notice in all this how the archetype of the assisting force has the power to cross generations. Jung, in *Memories, Dreams, Reflections*, refers to the unfinished tasks our ancestors have bequeathed to us:

I became aware of the fateful links between me and my ancestors. I feel very strongly that I am under the influence of things or questions which were left incomplete and unanswered by my parents and grandparents and more distant ancestors. It often seems as if there were an impersonal karma within a family, which is passed on from parents to children. It has always seemed to me that I had to answer questions which fate had posed to my forefathers, and which had not yet been answered, or as if I had to complete, or perhaps continue, things which previous ages had left unfinished.

In *A Blue Fire,* the psychologist James Hillman explores a related idea:

We are born into a family and, at the last, we rejoin its full extension when gathered to the ancestors. Family grave, family altar, family trust, family secrets, family pride. Our names are our family name, our physiognomies bear family traits and our dreams never let us depart from home— father and mother, brother and sister—from those faces and those rooms. Even alone and only ourselves, we are also always part of them, *partly them* [my italics].

Our ancestors—both those by DNA and those by lineage of similar spiritual or religious practice—ultimately give us a sense of *continuity*: we experience ourselves as part of a long line of earlier humans who have not only survived but have prepared a path for us. They may even have advanced the evolution of our species. Our place in line can certainly be important to those who arrive here after us, either by DNA or by lineage.

A GUIDE TO THE BEYOND

"Psychopomp" is a word from Greek meaning "guide of the soul"—another role of an assisting force. In classical mythology, the psychopomp is a spirit or deity who escorts people to the underworld when they die. In the Jungian view, a psychopomp thus symbolizes the link between conscious and unconscious. The psychopomp is the escort carrying the soul over the threshold between life and death. In this guise, the psychopomp is sometimes a ferryman—as in the case of Charon in Greek mythology. In Hindu religion, Shiva leads the soul to liberation after death. In Islam the role of psychopomp is played by the angel of death, Azrael. This same archetype appears in Talmudic tradition as the angel Samael. In Christianity, St. Michael is the escort and St. Peter greets the soul at the gates of heaven. Jizo bodhisattva is the equivalent ally archetype in Buddhism. A trustworthy psychotherapist is, in effect, also a psychopomp—escorting us into the vast and enigmatic world of our unconscious.

Sometimes the psychopomp appears in stories in the form of an animal such as a horse, dog, or bird. In some ancient traditions people believed that a flock of birds would gather outside the house of someone ready to pass beyond this mortal plane. They came to fly the dying to their spiritual home. Along these lines, people about to die might have dreams of dead relatives who seem to be beckoning them to the other side. This is also an example of the psychopomp archetype: the dead come to guide the dying to the next plane. In this context, Marie-Louise von Franz, in *On Dreams and Death*, spoke of dreams as psychopomps. She shared her realization about the possibility of a "next plane" this way: "All of the dreams of people facing death indicate that the unconscious, that is, our instinct world, prepares consciousness not for a definite end but for a profound transformation."

Closeness to death can also make us more aware of the power of love as we ourselves depart. Recently, I was struck by this touching Bible passage: "Now before the Feast of Passover, Jesus knew that the hour had come for him to leave this world and go to the Father. Having loved his own who were in the world, he loved them to the end" (John 13:1). I noticed that Jesus was combining closeness to death with loving more. Like any bodhisattva, he was facing his own ending with a commitment to an ongoing love of others—an impossible feat unless love is indeed everlasting and all that matters. From this passage, I made the connection between "death" and "ally" and "love."

I also thought of two other examples: When Aldous Huxley was on his deathbed, his wife asked him if there was any final question still on his mind. Aldous replied that he had only been wondering about one thing: how he could love her more. That is true caring for the beloved in one's last moments, rather than being shrouded in self-concern. It seems that *bodhicitta*, death-transcending dedication to others, had beautifully taken root in him. We see a deep spiritual sense of this also in the words of Plotinus, on his deathbed, to a friend: "I was waiting for you. I wanted to say good-bye before the divine in me departed to the divine in all."

Our allies who transcend death are not disembodied souls hovering over us but an energy-presence. We feel this presence especially in desolate or dire times. Many of us have experienced how it comes to us when needed, without our having to ask for it—a grace. A friend of mine told me of a dream in which his mother, who had not been kind to him in childhood, came to him after her death. She told him she was sorry for how she had treated him and wanted him to know she did indeed love him. It may take someone a long time to become the assisting force we had hoped they would have been all along.

In his poem "Frau Bauman, Frau Schmidt, and Frau Schwartze," Theodore Roethke describes three old caring women from his childhood:

Now, when I'm alone and cold in my bed,
They still hover over me,
These ancient leathery crones. . . .

Recently an older student asked me what I might suggest regarding preparing for death. This response immediately came to my mind (I trust from an assisting force): "We don't hold on too long or let go too fast." I then realized that we have always known how to do this: We were born on the day we were ready to make our personal appearance. We did not hold on too long so our birthday would come a day later, nor did we let go too soon so it would come a day earlier. (By the way I am writing this paragraph on January 14, my own birthday.)

Finally, we can consider a psychological phenomenon called "felt presence." Some climbers of Everest have reported a sense of an accompanying mountaineer-comrade when their trek is especially lonely and discouraging. The presence is not visible to the senses but feels authentic in a way that makes it unlike a delusion. The experience seems to reflect our longing for comfort in hard times. From a Jungian perspective, it is as if the higher Self chimes in when an experience has become monotonous or dead-ended or when we feel forlorn and desolate. Our ordinary sense of body-boundary blurs and we feel another presence by our side. Neuroscience-wise, this may reflect activity in the temporal-parietal junction, the insula and the frontoparietal cortex, parts of the brain that help integrate the activity of our senses including our body location and boundaries.

THE BUDDHIST LINEAGE

As we are now aware, our ancestors are not only our DNA relatives but any persons in our lineage of spiritual practice. In Buddhism, these ancestors are the Buddhas and bodhisattvas, enlightened beings who showed faithfulness to the Dharma and to actions of loving-kindness in their lifetime. They remain present and continue to assist us in those same two practices.

In *Beyond Thinking,* Dogen Zenji refers to the power of what in a religious context is called grace: "Buddha ancestors, out of their kindness, have opened the wide gate of compassion in order to let all sentient beings enter realization," he explains. "Those who think Buddhas appear only in the human realm have not yet entered the inner chambers of Buddha ancestors. . . . Shakyamuni in the heavenly realm teaches in far more varied ways, in one thousand styles, in ten thousand gates." Guidance from the ancestors is always tailored to our individual needs and paths.

We have seen that patron saints do not have to wait for us to come to them. They come to us when they see our need. This attentiveness to us reflects the style of the divine feminine ally Kuan Yin, who "hears the cries of those who suffer" and responds swiftly. All the bodhisattvas are drawn to us when they see us longing for enlightenment. Our move toward enlightened teachings and practices move our spiritual allies toward us—as do our sufferings.

Buddhist sutras continually offer invocations to the bodhisattvas. In the precepts ceremony (*jukai*), the practitioners chant in this touching way: "Om, *bodhisattva mahasattvas*, please concentrate your hearts on me." The initiates seek assistance from powers that offer what practices can't accomplish—the very definition of grace, the gift dimension of full spiritual consciousness. In *The Way of the Bodhisattva,* Shantideva prays to Manjushri, the bodhisattva of wisdom:

To you I bow,
Whose kindness is the wellspring of my good intent.
And to my virtuous friends I also bow
Whose inspiration gave me strength to grow.

We are indebted to the ancestors and can show gratitude. We are also indebted to posterity—indebted to those to whom we will be the ancestor allies. Our spiritual practices are how our debts to past generations are gladly paid and how our gifts are generously passed on to future generations. The ancient spiritual tools passed down to us give us a sense of continuity in our practices.

Ancestors speak to us; they ask us to continue the work they have done or finish the work they have left undone. There are no degrees of separation in the ongoing line of those in the human family who are committed to cocreating a world of justice, peace, and love. We inherited that task and are given the graces or assisting forces to help it happen. We must be careful not to become the kind of heirs who have forgotten or forfeited their inheritance. The gift doesn't go away though. Even a Johnny-come-lately will find it waiting, good as new.

PRACTICE

CONTEMPLATING OUR FOREBEARS

These three quotations from different traditions show our relationship to our spiritual and physical forebears and how those forebears accompany us now. Contemplate these quotations, and write down your thoughts about them.

I am ever dwelling in the presence of all the buddhas and bodhisattvas who are continually sharing their unobstructed vision.

—Shantideva

If I ever become a saint . . . I will be continually absent from heaven so I can bring light to those in darkness on earth.

—Mother Teresa

The believer in nonviolence has deep faith in the future. He knows that in his struggle for justice he has cosmic companionship. There is a creative force in this universe that works to bring the disconnected aspects of reality into a harmonious whole.

—Martin Luther King Jr.

WHEN AN ALLY DIES

When an important ally—a best friend, relative, partner, or mentor—dies, we know there is no one to fill the gap, no equivalent friend left. This adds weight to our mourning.

We realize that this friend had virtues and qualities we admired but did not so much see in ourselves. Such admiration is actually a positive projection: we can trust that we have those same qualities in ourselves but as untapped potential.

We also carry an image of any friend in our psyche the way we might carry a picture of a cherished person in a locket. We can use our active imagination to communicate, heartfully and mentally, to this friend's energy within us.

For some of us, the lost one is now looking after us from a realm beyond the visible world. For others it is an interior friend-energy that maintains the sense of contact. In honor of the departed friend, we might consider one or more of these spiritual practices. Each is a soulful way to celebrate the life of our lost friend and to keep our friend alive as long as we are alive.

- We identify at least three positive qualities we prized in our friend and affirm we will act them out in our own lives. The virtues of our friend have now become a legacy to us, and we are committing ourselves to pass this luminous inheritance on to others.

- We recall any unfinished emotional business that might be left between us. We acknowledge regrets for what we said or did that might have broken trust or caused pain of any kind. We acknowledge regrets for what we failed to say or do that would have shown our caring, committed connection. In our heart we feel contrition and may internally apologize. We can also write out our regrets and then burn the list as a ritual of closure, at the gravesite if appropriate.
- We occasionally talk silently or aloud (when we are alone) to our lost friend, who is now an assisting force, a bodhisattva, a guardian angel. We can see this practice as imaginative or real in accord with our own beliefs. The communication can include declaring our grief and our trust in an ongoing connection. We may express gratitude for all the wonderful times we had together. We may ask for ongoing assistance and guidance on our spiritual path. When St. Dominic was dying, he consoled his brother friars: "Do not weep, for I shall be more useful to you after my death and I shall help you then more effectively than during my lifetime."
- We recall the places in nature our friend loved most, and we go there to sit in silence with a sense of our friend's presence in and beside us. We then commemorate our friend with a ritual of our own making that combines gratitude, goodbye, and fidelity to our unending connection.

8 WHEN BUDDHA IS OUR REFUGE AND ALLY

[We are] . . . taking refuge in the Buddha as the example, in the dharma as the path, and in the sangha as companionship—giving up oneself, giving up one's stronghold.

—Chögyam Trungpa, *Training the Mind and Cultivating Loving-Kindness*

As we saw above, Buddhism offers three refuges—assisting forces—to us in times of trouble or at any time: the Buddha, the Dharma, and the Sangha. These refuges are known as the three jewels of an enlightened life—that is, the most valuable tools and stabilizing go-tos on life's sinuous trails. The Buddha as refuge refers both to the historical Buddha and to our own enlightened mind, always and already in us—that is, inherent in our nature, our primary assisting force. The Dharma is Buddha's enlightened teaching, an infallible guidance. The Sangha is the universal community of fellow practitioners of Buddhism, our companions on his Way.

All three refuges offer a safe place for us to go in times of depression, anxiety, and confusion. But they offer much more than a "place to go." They can also be trusted to offer restorative fulfillments of our deepest needs. Like ancestors and patron saints, they surround us with compassion after or even before we ask. They are on the lookout at all times, intent on devising ways to tailor their powers to our longings and sufferings. The Buddha, Dharma, and Sangha are continuously practicing loving-kindness toward all of us. The loving-kindness practice in Buddhism shows compassionate concern first for ourselves, then for our near and dear, and finally for all beings far and wide. We will present this practice in detail in our final chapter.

Another Buddhist practice is to take refuge in the three gems—Buddha, Dharma, Sangha—as a lifelong commitment to live in accord with what they represent. In this regard, we can recite a simple set of aspirations each day: "I take refuge in the Buddha. I take refuge in the Dharma. I take refuge in the Sangha." A refuge is a place of safety in times of peril, these times, any times.

The greatest perils to enlightenment are the three poisons: greed, hate, and the illusion of separateness. As we saw above, enlightened living includes freedom from greed in favor of generosity, freedom from hate in favor of love, and freedom from dualism and division in favor of oneness. When we turn to the Buddha, the Dharma, and the community of fellow pilgrims, we find a sanctuary from the three harmful poisons.

In the same refuges we also hear an invitation to practice the three alternative virtues. Each of the three poisons is an inherent inclination in all of us, so we need help not to fall into their snares. That help is the Buddha, the Dharma, and the Sangha:

- Greed is nullified by taking refuge in the Buddha's generosity in sharing the teachings with all of us; by taking refuge in the Dharma, which encourages generosity, and by taking refuge in the Sangha, which encourages us to share the teachings with one another.
- Hate is ended when we act in the world with the same universal caring, committed connection that motivated Buddha. In addition, it is offset by the Dharma of loving-kindness and the harmony of the community of practitioners.

- The illusion of separateness is dispelled when we realize all beings have the same Buddha nature, when we respect the Dharma of nonduality, and find like-heartedness in the Sangha.

We see the archetype of the assisting force at work especially in a reliable teacher of the Dharma. She is the one who guides and supports our practice without her own ego getting in the way. This sort of teacher is an example of a visible assisting force, a person who can be trusted to pilot us to the port of enlightenment— someone who has left ego behind and is not controlling us or demanding veneration of or dependence from us. We can recognize the true teacher-as-ally in someone who focuses only on our advancing in Buddhahood.

We also find an assisting force for our practice in the sutras and books written by teachers living or dead. We may not meet these teachers in person but they help us by the wisdom they share. This access to wisdom of course applies to any scripture or writing that contributes to our psychological or spiritual advancement, all sacred.

The root meaning of the word for Dharma is *support*. When we say "dharma gates are boundless," we mean there are assisting forces everywhere around us. Everything is supporting our move toward enlightened living. Dharma in the Mahayana tradition includes *bodhicitta*, personal commitment to supporting and aspiring to the enlightenment of others. Such a commitment represents an awakening to the purpose of life as not only about finding enlightenment for ourselves but also wanting it for all beings. In that sense, our commitment to bodhicitta is the same as our commitment to being an assisting force to all humanity.

Buddhas and bodhisattvas of the past and present are helping us now because of their bodhicitta vow to do so. In her essay "Becoming the Ally of All Beings," Sharon Salzberg points out: "All beings are connected: We are all bodhisattvas, not in the sense of being saviors running around taking care of everybody's problems, but through the truth of interconnectedness. There is no separation. We all belong to each other." Thus those who taught us to follow the path of nonviolence and loving-kindness, for instance, were always and already our allies. They showed us another reason why assisting forces are necessary: We might not have come up with the practice of loving-kindness toward those who have hurt us on our own. Without help, we might instead have believed that our cave-ancestor impulse to retaliate was our only option.

BODHISATTVA COMPANIONS

Buddha ancestors, out of their kindness, have opened the wide gate of compassion in order to let all sentient beings enter realization.

—Eihei Dogen Zenji, "On the Endeavor of the Way"

A bodhisattva is someone who has vowed not to enter nirvana until she has helped the rest of us find enlightenment. Some bodhisattvas are already enlightened; some are still engaged in spiritual practices that will definitely lead to enlightenment. Some bodhisattvas are living now; others are no longer alive. Both are considered assisting forces on our own voyage under the north star of illumination. We are actually all called to be bodhisattvas, helpers of humanity. The bodhisattva graces that come our way are meant to lead us to that goal. In most religious traditions, bodhisattvas are called "saints," which is what we are also called to become— and given the graces to be.

Bodhisattvas are personifications of enlightened energies around and in us. As we saw in the introduction, spiritual allies such as bodhisattvas are not to be configured as gods "out there" or in the sky. Joseph Campbell, in *The Hero with a Thousand Faces*, wrote,

The gods and goddesses then are to be understood as embodiments and custodians of the elixir of Imperishable Being but not themselves the Ultimate in its primary state. What the hero seeks through his intercourse with them is therefore not finally themselves, but their grace . . . the power of their sustaining substance. . . . The realm of the gods is a forgotten dimension of the world we know.

As we saw above, St. Thomas Aquinas taught that guardian angels were blind to religious affiliation—likewise, bodhisattvas help all beings, not just Buddhists. Bodhisattvas have all the qualities of the ally archetype: they are guides to enlightened living, helpers in times of struggle, and companions to those who suffer, especially those suffering by being caught in the illusion of separateness. In Mahayana Buddhism, a bodhisattva aspires to help and teach all beings the way to end suffering. Again we meet the important theme in the story of how allies help us: they show us how to be self-assisting forces and allies to others.

Bodhisattvas are committed to help all beings by sharing wisdom, compassion, and loving-kindness. They make this promise to us: "We choose to be a refuge for the world, a place of rest" (*Astasahasrika* 15–293). The *Prajnaparamita Sutra* adds, "The bodhisattvas will always maintain a motherly mind, consecrated to the constant protection, education, and maturing of conscious beings, inviting and guiding them along the path of all-embracing love."

As we keep seeing, spiritual truth is always and everywhere unanimous. The words of the Italian healer and saint Padre Pio in *The Great Promise* shows the same commitment in a religious context: "I asked for the grace of not entering paradise until all my spiritual children have entered first." The topic of assisting force is a hub, and people in all traditions and times are spokes all looking alike yet each with a unique spin.

FOUR BODHISATTVA FRIENDS

Let's contemplate the four main bodhisattvas in the Buddhist tradition: Samantabhadra, Manjushri, Avalokiteshvara, and Jizo. We will describe them as beings, but we keep in mind that they are more accurately *archetypes*, models of energies that are intrinsic to all of us. The bodhisattva energies reside in us only as potentials until we activate them through bodhicitta, our commitment to being the loyal allies of all beings on their path to enlightenment—that is, our commitment to working for the enlightenment of everyone. Bodhicitta has taken root in us by our practices of meditation, loving-kindness, wisdom, and compassion. Everything we read in this section about the bodhisattvas describes what *we* truly are and what we can activate with practice.

Samantabhadra

Samantabhadra is the all-good bodhisattva of enlightened action working in the world of today. He is especially associated with the interconnection, the kinship of all beings. It is he who helps us with our Buddhist practices, especially meditation. Samantabhadra is also the guardian of the *Lotus Sutra*. He is the patron guardian of Sri Lanka, another example of a bodhisattva as the archetype of the assisting force.

Samantabhadra has made the following vows on our behalf: showing honor to all Buddhas, praising all Buddhas, making generous offerings, confessing and repenting misdeeds, rejoicing about the joy of others, asking for the Dharma teachings, studying the Dharma, requesting all Buddhas to remain in the world and keep teaching us, following Buddha's teaching to help all beings, forgoing nirvana until all beings can join too, and passing his own merits on to others. All of the vows somehow fit the helper archetype.

Samantabhadra is thought to be hidden in our puzzling world in forms we may never fully recognize. In this he is the archetype of the invisible assisting force, the *secret* helper. Such unknown sources of spiritual assistance are exemplified, for instance, in the effect on us of the aspirations of the thousands of practitioners today who are asking that all beings be happy. We don't know who they are but they are our allies, aspiring for our happiness and liberation. We see this same unknown source of assistance in the many people in the world who pray for or engage in spiritual practices for the benefit of all of us, yet we never notice or meet them.

Here we see how universal gratitude is a spiritual practice. It acknowledges the benefits that are coming our way from so many helpers and spiritual friends, even when unknown. Sir Walter Scott, in the novel *Rob Roy*, notes, in this charming way, how we can trust a secret helper: "If danger was around me . . . how could I learn its nature, or the means of averting it, but by meeting my unknown counselor, to whom I could see no reason for imputing any other than kind intentions."

The help we are receiving is not limited to those who aspire or pray for us. In so many areas of our lives unknown or forgotten allies, silently and humbly, exert influence on us and on our sincere practice: Right now I, David, am still benefiting from all the love others have shown me over the course of my lifetime. I am sharing what I found out from so many teachers, Buddhist and otherwise. I am daring to write what I think I know thanks to all the friends and teachers who taught and encouraged me. And you are reading and hopefully benefiting from what I write thanks to those who taught and encouraged you. All were and are showing both of us what assisting forces are all about—and that will always be what we are called to be.

Manjushri

Manjushri is the bodhisattva of *prajna*, transcendent wisdom—that is, wisdom beyond what the linear mind can attain. His name translates as "gentle glory," though he is pictured brandishing a fiery double-edged sword in his right hand. The sword-in-hand is a metaphor for his vow to cut through our ego ferociously and, without hesitation or exception, to sever our attachment to division and duality. This liberatory "cutting through," like the gifts of all the bodhisattvas, is something we would not likely do on our own! We see now so clearly how *essential* is the work of assisting forces if we are to grow to our full spiritual stature. Egos need help to let go. Humans need help to be human.

The sword of Manjushri can be seen as an equivalent of the lightsaber given to Luke Skywalker by his assisting force, Obi-Wan Kenobi, in *Star Wars*. The same weapon that cuts through ego-centeredness can be the assisting force that helps us wield it for the good of an entire galaxy!

Manjushri also focuses us on the teaching of emptiness—that is, the teaching that nothing is freestanding, including us. All is connected; nothing has an inherent separate existence, especially not our own egos. In this capacity, Manjushri keeps us safe from imbibing the poison of illusion.

In his left hand Manjushri holds a lotus, on which is written the *Prajnaparamita Sutra*, signifying the full realization of wisdom. Manjushri sits on a lion, a metaphor for how fiercely he is devoted to taming our ego so it can open to supreme wisdom. All this helps us see how the archetype of the assisting force has a hard edge sometimes. Indeed, it may be that only hard knocks will open the ego-locked door of our hearts. Manjushri knows so well that the piratical individualism of ego can blockade the argosy of enlightenment that wants to sail our way. He never gives up on helping us welcome it.

Manjushri is venerated both as Vagishvara, "Lord of Speech," and as Manjughosha, "the melodious-voiced." He thus not only gives us wisdom but the power to express it in eloquent and artistic ways. In yet another dimension of Manjushri's domain, he is the patron of astrologers, showing how his help extends beyond the limits of the individual mind into the far reaches of the galaxies. In this capacity he folds the finite into the infinite, another joyous grace to us.

Avalokiteshvara

The familiar smiling Avalokiteshvara is the bodhisattva of pure and universal compassion. He hears the cries of suffering of all beings and responds to all of them. Since bodhisattvas simultaneously help us and demonstrate our practice, this hearing and responsiveness by Avalokiteshvara shows us our calling. We too are here to listen to the cries of those who are treated unjustly, for instance, and to respond with social change-making compassion. We take our stand against the oppressive forces, the afflicting forces, that bring suffering to us, other humans, and the planet. When we do this, Avalokiteshvara has found yet another way to be alive today. Each of us can give any bodhisattva or saint that opportunity. In fact, this is one of the reasons we were given a lifetime.

Avalokiteshvara is often pictured with many arms and with an eye in the palm of each hand. This representation symbolizes how he reaches out into all the universe and sees every form of suffering—always with a will to end it. Recall that bodhisattvas, like patron saints, don't wait for our aspirations and prayers. They anticipate our needs, even being aware of them before we are. We remind ourselves again that we are not talking literally here but metaphorically. In all our descriptions of the bodhisattvas we are describing what happens in us when we open.

Avalokiteshvara is venerated as the assistant of Amitabha, the heavenly Buddha in the Pure Land tradition of Buddhism. Together, Avalokiteshvara and Amitabha continually teach the Dharma. We see the characteristics of the ally archetype in how Avalokiteshvara combines the roles of being an assistant to Amitabha and being a compassionate responder to us in our suffering.

We see these same qualities in His Holiness the Dalai Lama, loyal ally of humanity, who is believed to be an incarnation of the bodhisattva Avalokiteshvara.

The Japanese word *myoshi* is often associated with Avalokiteshvara. It means "mysterious help," a definition that fits with the hidden-assistance element that we saw in the archetype of Samantabhadra. And again, what the bodhisattvas give us we are called to give others. Our daily practice of aspiring for happiness for all beings everywhere makes us hidden helpers for the benefit of all beings.

In China, Avalokiteshvara is Kuan Yin, a feminine form of the bodhisattva known as "Goddess of Mercy." We recall that the Virgin Mary is known as "Mother of Mercy," showing the universality of the feminine dimension of the archetype of compassion. Kuan Yin is also depicted with a thousand hands and eleven faces, demonstrating her capacity for responding to each unique need suffering humans may have—the same style as that of Avalokiteshvara.

Tara, considered a feminine emanation of Avalokiteshvara, is the most popular Tibetan Buddhist version of that bodhisattva. The white Tara has a third eye in her forehead, representing the way in which she is ever intent on visualizing humanity and its needs and then being generously responsive to us. She is also trusted to give good fortune. The green Tara holds lotus flowers and is believed to bring us wisdom, especially through art. These two, along with all the other Taras—twenty-one altogether in the Tibetan tradition—are believed to be continually helping us. In images of Taras, their breasts are exposed, an expression of their commitment to nurturing us. One of their hands is raised in blessing and the other offers us sanctuary—all exemplifications of the archetype of the ally.

As I write this section I feel a bodily resonance with and visceral awe at the supreme wisdom and inexhaustible generosity of the Buddhist teaching on bodhisattvas. To tell us of allies all around us, to assure us we can trust them as refuges to turn to and as guardians who watch over us—what splendid gifts. And all the gifts are being bestowed on us without our having to merit them. The Dharma is so utterly spectacular!

Jizo

Ksitigarbha is the Sanskrit name of the bodhisattva known in Japan as Jizo. He vowed to teach the Dharma and not to find enlightenment for himself until he emptied all the hell realms of their suffering captives. He is pictured as a monk with a halo carrying a staff that he will use to break through the gates of hell. Jizo also holds a "wish-fulfilling gem" that he uses to dispel the darkness of ignorance. He protects children and travelers, so his statues are often placed at crossroads or on the banks of a river. Notice that both of these are realms of the "between," the spiritual space in which we do not have to take an action, only open to the assisting forces that will invariably show us the next step. Jizo helps us in such transitions, the liminal times in life when we most need an ally.

Jizo is also a guide and conductor to the afterlife, a psychopomp. In Buddhist wisdom and teaching, an afterlife is only an opportunity to continue our practice of loving-kindness toward all beings and to remain loyal to our commitment to cocreate a world of justice, peace, and love. For what other reason would we want an afterlife? We recall the words of St. Therese (a bodhisattva indeed): "I will spend my heaven doing good on earth." She does not ask to receive a reward after death—only the chance to go on giving to others. This commitment to humanity is central to the archetype of the assisting force and, as with all its characteristics, our calling too. We find out what we are here to do by observing what the holy ones do for us.

Jizo is especially venerated as a "patron of the impossible." When we face our worst predicaments and are besieged with apparently insurmountable hardships, Jizo steps in to support us. He highlights a most significant feature of the ally archetype:

reliability, no matter how overwhelming the circumstances or how dense the barricades. Our human practice and purpose follow this same bodhisattva quality: We stand pat with those who suffer. We do not shrink back because of the fearsomeness of the adversity around us. We remain faithful and courageous allies of humanity.

Jizo's vow to assist all beings extends so far as to include a commitment to take the place of people in their miseries and misfortunes. In this he becomes our exemplar of valiant compassion, giving even one's life for others, a quality viewed as heroism in society and as sanctity in religion. Jizo, like all bodhisattvas, never asks for reciprocation. This selfless compassion is yet another quality of the assisting force archetype.

Jizo knows how hard life can be and feels sympathy for our human plight. He knows how hard it is to stay faithful to our practices. To succor us in this situation, the compassionate Jizo remains steadfastly present to us in times of suffering. Indeed, Jizo stands with us, stands in for us, stands by us—but never does he become contaminated by our confusions or sufferings. He relates to human travail but does not become so caught in it that he is no longer capable of helping us. Like the wounded healer, he is wounded with us but not hobbled by our wounds or his.

In Jizo's approach to compassion we see a crucial feature of the healthy ally archetype as it applies to us: we are called to help but at the same time to safeguard our own health and sanity. Our bodies and minds are our vehicles for the practicing of our calling to alliance and compassion, always found together. It is a psychological and spiritual practice therefore to respect these instruments, to keep them safe and useful. We take care of ourselves while—and so that—we can also help others effectively. Indeed, the loving-kindness practice names us as its first beneficiaries!

Along these lines, we can distinguish empathy from compassion. In empathy we feel what the other feels. In compassion we feel *for* what the other feels. To help effectively, we need to be fully compassionate while modulating our empathy. We care about the suffering of others and want to help them find release from it. But we protect ourselves from becoming possessed by their pain, from being drawn into it so much that it incapacitates us—which is the path to burnout.

Finally, we remind ourselves that the main thrust of bodhisattva practice is bodhicitta—wanting enlightenment in order to help others find it too. We can't reach bodhicitta when we are primarily dedicated to promoting our own happiness. Bodhicitta happens only in the context of our commitment to be of ongoing service to humanity and to the planet on which it stands. Such a wonderful commitment shows us once more how an archetype such as a bodhisattva is both an ally and an exemplar of our own marvelous spiritual destiny: I am here to display in time the timeless design of love and service that is in me. I trust that whatever happens to me is part of how my calling to be an assisting force in the world is unfolding. I trust that nothing that happens to me can cancel my commitment to this splendid destiny. And I honor the timing all this takes.

Now we can look once more at the main gifts of the four bodhisattvas to see exactly how they are assisting forces on our journey to enlightenment:

- Samantabhadra gives us penetrating awareness of our universal kinship.
- Manjushri cuts through our ego's inveterate habits of division and dualism.
- Avalokiteshvara invites and activates our universal compassion.
- Jizo shows us how to commit ourselves to a life of loving service.

As we know, the four bodhisattvas are not persons; they are personifications, metaphors for a spiritual reality. Metaphor in this context is not simply a comparison of two unlike things. It is the "more than" words or personifications can convey, the depth-reality behind what appears to be only a surface. The bodhisattvas are thus depictions of a highly significant fact about the path to enlightenment: we can't get on the path alone; we can't traverse it alone; we can't complete it alone. We are enlightened in our Buddha nature. But turning that enlightenment into action requires ingredients we don't have on our own. We need to receive them—another example of the necessity of the assisting force archetype in any human story. Thus bodhisattva energy shows us the necessity of grace, the gift dimension of life—precisely what the assisting force archetype is about.

The four bodhisattvas illustrate the connection between practice, effort, and gift: To live an enlightened life of joy and wisdom, we need "more than" whatever we ourselves can know or do. We need bodhisattva help and graces to supplement what we bring to the table. On our own, for instance, we would not "ferociously" cut through dualism. We need ruthless help for that, personified by Manjushri. This same reliance applies to each of the specific graces of the bodhisattvas. We can't "do it all." Yet, it all can happen because a steadfast assisting force is handing itself to us every day and right now—the whole universe is joining in with us to let there be light.

PRACTICE

A WEEK OF PRACTICE

Below are seven quotations, one for every day of the week. Read a quotation each day, copy it out in your own handwriting, and then post it where you can see it throughout the day. Ponder it and record your thoughts and feelings about it by writing them down. Create an affirmation that shows how the quotation can activate itself in your life. Write a reply to any or all of the three questions following each quotation. Look back at all you wrote in a month. Repeat the practice as often you like.

Sunday

Waking or sleeping
In a grass shack,
I pray
To carry others across
Before myself.

—Eihei Dogen Zenji, *Waka Poems*

Who in your life has carried you, when you needed that, and how are you grateful to that person?

Whom have you carried and how are you grateful for the grace to have done or now be doing that?

How do you carry and put others first without disregarding your own legitimate needs?

Monday

The bodhisattva says yes to the most evil world, for he knows himself to be one with it. . . . Thus he must love all beings as he loves himself, but he cannot rest until everyone mirrors divinity in everything. The bodhisattva, not the sage, embodies the aim of human aspiration.

—Hermann Keyserling, *The Travel Diary of a Philosopher*

How can you realistically recognize the fact of evil in the world and see it potentially in yourself too, rather than only "out there"?

What does "the divine" mean to you and what will it take for you to see it in yourself and in all things?

What is your highest aspiration, the longing in your higher Self, and how do your spiritual practices help you fulfill it?

Tuesday

The one intention is to have a sense of gentleness toward others and a willingness to be helpful to others always. That seems to be the essence of the bodhisattva vow. In whatever you do . . . have the attitude of being of benefit to all beings.

—Chögyam Trungpa, *Training the Mind and Cultivating Loving-Kindness*

How can the following vow become real in your life: "No matter how others treat me, I always choose the path of gentle love"?

What needs to change in your attitude toward others so that your whole life purpose is to be of benefit to them?

Who are the people in your life today who help you live as a bodhisattva and vice-versa?

Wednesday

Bodhisattvas do not become liberated from life, nor do they pursue any form of separate self-realization. They direct an ecstatic flood of love and friendliness toward all, connecting their mind streams as intimately with all beings as with their most cherished family member and beloved friend. This astonishing spiritual feat frees the bodhisattvas from every impure intention of harming, denigrating, abandoning or even merely ignoring others.

—Lex Hixon, *Mother of the Buddhas: Meditation on the Prajnaparamita Sutra*

How can you open yourself to the flow of love that ceaselessly courses through you and let it reach all beings?

What intention to harm or to bring about suffering to others awaits your amends or transformation?

How can you advance in cherishing all beings in more personally friendly ways?

Thursday

Bodhisattvas show the love that is truly a refuge for all beings, the love that is serene because it is free of grasping or compulsion, the love that is rooted in reality because it abides in equanimity, the love that is free of expectation because it is not caught in attachment or aversion.

—Vimalakirti Sutra

At the times when you are willing to be totally candid with yourself, whom or what do you turn to for refuge in times of trouble?

What are the ways you may still be caught in grasping and compulsion and how can you let go of them?

What change in yourself will help you toward equanimity in the midst of your daily stresses and challenges?

Friday

The bodhisattvas will always maintain a motherly mind, consecrated to the constant protection, education, and maturing of conscious beings, inviting and guiding them along the path of all-embracing love.

—Prajnaparamita Sutra

How can you awaken to what keeps guiding you along the path that leads to an all-embracing love?

How can you consecrate yourself to cocreating a world of justice, peace, and love?

How is your spiritual practice deepening your own unique way of loving?

Saturday

Although we practice with people, our goal is to practice with mountains and rivers, with trees and stones, with everything in the world, everything in the universe, and to find ourselves in this big cosmos. . . . [Then] we know intuitively which way to go.

—Shunryu Suzuki, *Not Always So*

How can you find in nature a path to inner peace?

What helps you awaken to the presence of Buddha, enlightened energy, in the natural world?

How are the moon and stars alive in you as reflections of your Buddhist nature?

COMPLETING THE PRACTICE

At the end of this week of practices, and on each day for the next week or more, you may want to recite this paraphrase of and expansion on the Mahayana Buddhist full moon ritual:

All my ancient and twisted karma
from beginningless greed, hate, and ignorance
—born of body, speech, and mind—
I now fully avow, repent, and won't repeat.
By a wonderful grace
I am converted to Buddha's way,
the path of integrity and loving-kindness
and a refuge from every fear.
I bow in profound thanks to my spiritual allies.
I trust their presence in every here and now of my life.

HOW MEDITATION CAN BE AN ASSISTING FORCE

A refuge is anything we keep coming back to for respite or safety. Whatever we keep coming back to for help is an ally. When we return to consciousness of our breath in mindfulness meditation, we are finding help in remaining focused. Our breath has become an ally—not only by refocusing us away from distractions. Mindful focus on our breath can likewise lead us to two important teachings. First, as we let our thoughts come and go without getting caught in entertaining or repelling them, we are experiencing impermanence. Second, we come to see that we are not a solid, separate, lasting self. We are then a breath closer to enlightenment.

PRACTICE
A "REALITY BREATH" PRACTICE

This practice is not aimed at using the breath to bring us back to mindful focus but instead is simply aimed at regulating our breath to match a circumstance, especially a challenging one. As an example, we are anxious: we attend to our anxious breath, simply noticing it, granting it hospitality, not trying to calm it. Thus *we bring our breath to honor what is rather than using it to cancel what is.* Each breath becomes a yes to our tense predicament. Now we are present in the moment in a fearless and grounded way. This tailored breath awareness helps us live through a crisis with equanimity. Breath is an assisting force when that happens. We are finding yet another way by which events can be opportunities for practice and for healing. We are aligning a life event with an opportunity for mindfulness—achieving presence in the here and now without trying to change anything. Yet in fact change happens, because we move from stress to serenity in the long run.

We can use reality-breath meditation as a skillful means to handle a mood or issue. It is a way of recollecting and anchoring ourselves. Now we are residing in the moment, the best position from which to open our capacity for equanimity. In mindfulness we let go of preferences such as serenity rather than anxiety. In this practice, as in mindfulness, it is not that we don't have any preferences—it is just that our preferences can't stop or drive us.

We are actually applying the five A's—attention, affection, appreciation, acceptance, allowing—to the circumstances that are happening in our life, and even to our own resistance. Since another given of life is resistance, a yes to that is still a form of surrender, albeit provisional and preliminary. Saying yes to what is opens us to what comes next. Trusting that sequence is the first step required on our heroic journey. Later, by having said yes to our simply standing on the dock, we are more likely to dive in.

PRACTICE

ALERT SITTING PRACTICE

In the following practice by which we feel a spiritual assisting force at work, we are practicing *alert sitting*—letting our mind do what it does and observing it without having to keep coming back to our breaths or back to a specific focus. In this meditation style, we are not making ourselves toe the line, not making ourselves engage in what others may define as "proper meditation technique." This practice involves silent sitting along the lines of sitting in a theater watching a play or film: you allow the actors to do what they do with no attempt to get them to do what you believe they should do. In this sense, alert sitting and mindfulness are practices of nonviolence, a nonaggressive stance toward reality.

In mindfulness meditation, we abide in consciousness of the present moment impartially and fearlessly. Since time is a continual interplay of impermanence and evolving, to be present in the moment is to be in the flow of time, never static. We focus our awareness on our breath—which is always moving through us and, like time, is never static. To be in the now is not to be on hold. It is "to be still and still moving," as T. S. Eliot said. Flow joins in with flux.

Such alert awareness is a practice of "more than" mindfulness: we open our meditation into a daily style of seeing more into things and happenings. For instance, our contemplative gaze at a visible object, especially in nature, ushers us into a deeper dimension of it. We see the interior liveliness of something and our gaze is appreciative. Henry David Thoreau experienced this kind of visioning in nature, writing in his journal: "If by watching all day and all night, I may detect some trace of the ineffable, then will it not be worth the while to watch?"

Deep attention reveals paradox—and options too. For instance, in a relationship, we may find ourselves wanting freedom to do what we want and refusing to acknowledge the limits that are necessary in a committed bond. In alert attention—that is, with a deeper look—we see that they can coexist satisfactorily. Yet if all we have is bare mindfulness, those opposites may stay put in our perception as opposites—and keep stressing us and our relationships too.

With this wider mindful-contemplative consciousness, we can come to trust that the "real" is more than whatever is happening right in front of us in the moment—much more. When we keep looking at the manifest, we may miss the latent treasure. The treasure that is not so evident—but is reachable if we are open—is the "many splendored thing," the mystery, richness, and depth. This treasure is the sacred as sacramental—that is, signified externally yet reflecting what is happening in our own deepest psychic structures. In other words, some experiences, images, or natural phenomena hold a transformative power if we look deeply enough.

Perhaps a key to seeing how all this comes together is to contrast and then combine the concepts called "emptiness" in Zen and "fullness" in Hinduism. In Zen, since there is no separate self, what matters is paying attention to here-and-now reality and calming our impulses toward grasping and avoiding. In mindfulness meditation we are, in effect, emptying our minds of illusions and thereby we are reducing our suffering. Mindfulness helps us do this and can calm us down too.

Hinduism starts with a completely different premise: that everything is teeming with a divine presence. The purpose of calming down and paying attention is to become aware of this divine presence as reflective of the richness in one's own true nature. Mindfulness is a useful door, but it is important to walk through it if we are find the treasure that awaits us behind it. When we refresh and expand primary mindfulness with a sense of the awesome in all we face or see, our meditation practice takes on a whole new cast. Instead of just a space inside us we notice a burgeoning spaciousness. The empty was only empty so it could usher in the full.

By engaging in an alert sitting practice, we can move from the simple here-and-now-focused mindfulness style of meditation and enter into an X-ray vision of all that is in front of us—into an awe at its sacredness, its luminosity, its summons to us. We might then say, "I want to know what awaits me beyond the here-and-now veneer. In this combination of mindfulness and deep gazing the *here and now* becomes *hear and bow*."

Month by month, things are losing their hardness; even my body now lets the light through.

—Virginia Woolf, *The Waves*

9 WHEN WE BECOME THE ALLIES

O that my priest's robes were wide enough
To gather all the sufferings
Of this floating world.

                                    —Taigu Ryokan

All of us have longings. We long for help; we long to be of help. The helper energy, working in both directions, will be necessary for us if we are ever to be fulfilled. Needing help and being of help are not like frosting on a cake. They are necessary ingredients in how we humans collaborate to access wholeness and enlightenment. "In order to survive, all mortal beings need one another . . . passing on life's torch, like relay runners in a race," wrote the Roman philosopher Lucretius. Our human journey is indeed a relay race, successful only when we both receive from someone and give to someone. One of the most beautiful consequences of our receiving assistance from others is that it encourages us to be there for others too. Compassion does not stop at one-to-one; it becomes one-to-next. It is all relay after all, isn't it, this human round-robin?

It may take years to comprehend our spiritual calling to help others as we were helped. We have always known about heroes who achieved this important human possibility, but it may take years of our lives to see it also as our own personal destiny. In high school in the 1950s I read *The Catcher in the Rye*. Holden Caulfield, a character so wounded himself, wants to be someone who rescues children from falling off a cliff. I remember now that I admired his having that as a life purpose.

Only very recently did I grasp, for the first time, that Holden wanted to be nothing less than an *assisting force*. In addition, I realized that he personifies the archetype of the wounded healer. It took my writing of this book to realize what that novel I read so many years ago was really about. I keep noticing that synchronicity, memories, and new realizations are assisting forces too.

The assisting force that Holden Caulfield wanted to be is what we are here to be. We were in the rye near the cliff many times in life, but we were caught in someone's arms before we fell off the edge. It can be precisely the warm presence of assisting forces that arouses our desire to become present in that same way to others. Indeed, noticing how others have been allies to us over the years is how we learn to be allies too. We learn to give by noticing what we are given. I suppose, therefore, that the children Holden might have saved would themselves someday be catchers in the rye.

To be an assisting force in society, however, will take courage. We will have to stand up for justice at our own risk. We will have to speak truth to power. We may even have to lose a friend, a benefit, or a freedom we valued. It follows then that when we build our courage by working on letting go of our fears, we are building the inner resources we will need to be world allies. In fact, anything we do to build our healthy inner resources is equipping us to become more effective assisting forces all around.

Look where our personal journey to find support can lead us: We move from leaning on others to letting them lean on us. Indeed, we are not here only to live but to find something to live for—and that something is loving-kindness toward all beings, thereby cocreating a world of justice, peace, and love. The assisting-force energy in us becomes compassion when we are touched by any suffering being. True compassion is indiscriminate—that is, not based on what tugs the heartstrings and what doesn't. Our compassion, like our loving-kindness, extends both to victim and persecutor—as does our courage to stand up for the former and stand up to the latter.

Service is thus our spiritual practice. "Self-actualizing people are, without exception, involved in a cause outside their own skin, in something outside themselves," wrote the psychologist Abraham Maslow. "They are devoted to something, working at something . . . which is very precious to them—some calling or vocation in the old sense, the priestly sense. They are working on something which fate has called them to somehow and which they love." And, of course, fate can be an ally when we bow to its call or defy its obstacles.

But what if we are ourselves confused or inadequate? Can we still help others? This questions returns us to the archetype of the wounded healer: the character who has his or her own plaguing bruises and traumas but still manages to join in the healing of others. One does *not* have to be sane, stable, or even sensible to be an assisting force—as so many stories show. The clown, the fool, the outcast are characters who can still become providers of assistance to the hero or heroine. In our own lives, there are people we have known, or may now know, who are on the spectrum of being neurotic or even psychotic. Yet perhaps they have been bravura assisting forces to us nonetheless. There are also teachers, poets, and artists from whom we have gained much wisdom and courage, yet they themselves might have had serious mental health issues. That did not get in the way of their being assisting forces to us. And the same concept applies to us as helpful allies of others. We may have problems, but that does not stop us from being there for others when assistance has become our calling. As the journalist Charles Blow writes in his memoir *Fire Shut Up in My Bones*, "I wanted to stop caring but I couldn't. A heart still works even when it's broken."

The fact that people can be helped even by those who themselves need help reminds us that the wounded healer–assisting force archetype works well no matter who is its host—because ultimately the assisting force is grace. Help and alliance then come not *from* humans but *through* them. And no one is a reservoir of grace, although anyone can be its channel.

Help as one adult assisting force to another is not rescuing. Being of help does not mean fixing something for someone, solving it, making it go away. Help is also not necessarily taking the side of others; it is only being *at* their side. Sometimes it is only pointing the way, not being the way. It is staying *with* others as they walk through the haunted valley.

COMMITMENT TO ENLIGHTENMENT

Enlightenment is a mystery, only somewhat definable. We can, however, discuss what results when we practice enlightenment, how it manifests itself in our lifestyle, how it activates a commitment to become an assisting force. Enlightened living will entail wisdom in our choices, loving compassion in our relationships, and equanimity in the midst of our struggles and stresses. The word "enlightenment," taken literally, can also refer to a "lightening up" from the weight of our compulsions and anxieties, lightening our heavy-duty ego, the narcissistic ego that prevents us from waking up to our own true nature.

We can also ponder the implied meaning of enlightenment by considering its four qualities: loving-kindness, compassion, empathic joy, and equanimity. Since Brahma, divine creative energy, dwells (*vihara*) in all four qualities, they are known as *brahmaviharas*, the "abodes of the divine." The brahmaviharas are also called "the four immeasurables" because they signify a limitless and unconditional expressions of the four qualities. The personified god Brahma is believed to have four faces, reflecting each of those qualities. Put another way, each of the faces represents one of four ways of being an assisting force to humanity. They are inherent capacities in each one of us. Our challenge is to engage each of these in our choices and behavior.

When we practice the four immeasurables, we let go of some our primitive inclinations such as greed, hate, or the desire for revenge. We find we can make choices that take us beyond such instincts. Each of the four qualities of enlightenment becomes active in us through practice:

- Love becomes our antidote to indifference. This loving friendliness is the central quality of an awakened practitioner—and of the ally archetype.
- Active compassion offsets the sentimental pity that makes us seem to be above others.
- Joy at others' success frees us from envy.
- Equanimity keeps us even-tempered in the midst of stressful triggers.

In Buddhism the four brahmaviharas are also spiritual powers. This requires some muscle and courage if we are to practice them. In keeping with the word "immeasurable," we are enjoined to love *all* beings, another koan. It takes pluck and perseverance to show compassion toward all who suffer, to feel joy at others' good fortune, to maintain equanimity in the face of distress or disaster—all challenges indeed.

The brahmaviharas as graces on our spiritual path are assisting forces because they also *endow* us with the very strength and bravery we seek to practice. The four immeasurables enable us to live up to what a companion who is an ally does:

- In loving-kindness we extend unconditional friendliness to others.
- In compassion we not only feel for those who suffer but we also work on ending the injustices that are the causes of their suffering.

- In shared joy we celebrate others' success and thus form a closer bond with them. (The opposite is the envy that distances and divides us.)
- In equanimity we treat all people as equal and exhibit calmness and clarity in all circumstances. This evenness equips us to be of help as a voice of sanity in stressful times.

Regarding "shared joy," I am reminded of St. Paul: "Rejoice with those who rejoice; grieve with those who grieve" (Romans 12:15). Based on this, I am expanding my own sense of what the bramavihara recommends so that it becomes "I let myself feel *both* the joy and suffering of others." Now the practice combines happiness at others' good fortune with comourning of their misfortunes, a form of compassion. Thus, the first three bramaviharas are indeed one: loving-kindness, compassion, shared joy/shared suffering. Our calm and calming equanimity is the graced result.

Our practice of the four immeasurably beneficial qualities of enlightenment also draws helper-bodhisattvas to us. They see us doing what they did and collaborate with us to strengthen our resolve and boost the power of our practices. Thich Nhat Hanh, in *Guide to Walking Meditation,* writes about how our compassion invites accompaniment: "You will suffer with all beings, in kinship, as you feel the compassion of an awakening person, a *bodhisattva.* Then all those you encounter along the path, loving and peaceful or not, will likewise be *bodhisattvas,* your companions on the way."

Help is not on the way; help is the Way.
                    —Dairyu Michael Wenger, calligraphy-painting title

OUR VOWS TO BE ALLIES OF HUMANITY

"Rather than focusing on some future endpoint" (when all will be perfect), writes David R. Loy in *A New Buddhist Path,* "the bodhisattva vow indicates a *direction* to one's life, an undertaking that answers the ultimate question about the focus and meaning of life right here and now." The bodhisattva vow is fourfold:

- Beings are numberless; I vow to save them all.
- Delusions are inexhaustible; I vow to end them all.
- Dharma gates are boundless; I vow to enter them all.
- Buddha's way is unsurpassable; I vow to become it.

We notice, first of all, that these vows are riddles, commitments to fulfill what is impossible to fulfill. The reason the vows are stated this way is to free us from the logical, linear style of our thinking brain. Here they are restated with oxymoronic humor:

- If beings are numberless, we cannot save them all.
- Since delusions are inexhaustible, we will never be able to end them all.
- Since dharma gates are boundless, how could we possibly enter all of them?
- To aver that Buddha's way is unsurpassable means we can never fully traverse it, let alone become it.

But wait! Our vows don't have to be affirmations but rather they can be *aspirations*.

- We aspire to being assisting forces to all beings.
- We aspire to let go of our delusions, especially the one that denies the need for assisting forces.
- We aspire to find and enter whatever gate into the Dharma may open before us each day.
- We aspire to follow Buddha's way to whatever extent we can.

In the first vow, we feel compassion for suffering beings everywhere and we can't help but want to soothe them all. We love humanity so much we want to be there for suffering humans at a heart level. (This, and all four vows, are longings to be in the world as someone who cares about it in a connected, committed way—the very ingredients of love.)

In the second vow, we realize that delusions are inexhaustible and will plague us all our lives. We know our attitudes and actions will never fully align with reality. We know we will never be safe from deluding thoughts, plans founded on fantasies, cravings for things that are impossible to attain. Yet bravely we promise ourselves that we will not give up; we will keep engaging in the work of bringing delusions to an end.

In the third vow, we know that openings into the power and wisdom of the Dharma are infinite. We know in our logical minds that there is no prospect of gaining entrance through every one of its gates. Yet, audaciously, we vow to enter them all. We make the impossible sound possible, a humorous style that is itself one of the dharma gates.

In the fourth vow, we recognize that Buddha's energy is fully in us but putting our Buddha nature into practice fully is not within human reach. To say "I vow to become Buddha's way" is therefore not at all a commitment anyone can logically make. Yet we pay no attention to the limits; we transgress them with a twinkling eye. We work toward what can't work. We keep aspiring to navigate the impassable way as best we can and we call that a successful commitment. Then the purity of our intention turns out to be enough. Success in our spiritual practice has taken on a new definition: not "did it perfectly" but "did my best."

The bodhisattva vows are technologies by which we can evolve into assisting forces. The bodhisattva vows make us people who show up in times when people need us because they, like us, need release from suffering, attachment, delusion, ignorance, and un-enlightened choices. The vows hold not the slightest judgment against those who mess up over and over. We know how hard the path to becoming a healthy enlightened person is, especially since we ourselves are tripping on it so often.

Thus we are vowing to accomplish the impossible—and we are not the ones who could accomplish it anyway. We are ones who need allies to help us! Now we see why humor is a feature of all four of the humanly impossible vows. Yet we can still delight in such droll ironies. The bodhisattva vows are steps, not arrivals. Our daily attempt to fulfill them even in minor ways serves as our totally successful practice to become assisting forces to the human family and the planet where it lives. So the vows reflect our human calling. Joan Halifax states this idea perfectly in her foreword to Dan Leighton's *Faces of Compassion*: "What are we vowing, other than to be who we really are?"

PRACTICE

A LOVING-KINDNESS PRACTICE

Arthur Schopenhauer, in his major work on ethics *The Basis of Morality*, writes,

> When once compassion is stirred within me by another's pain then his weal and woe go straight to my heart. This happens exactly in the same way, if not always to the same degree, as otherwise I feel only my own. Consequently the difference between myself and the other is no longer an absolute one. . . . Compassion is an undeniable fact of human consciousness, an essential part of it, and does not depend on assumptions, conceptions, religions, dogmas, myths, training, and education. On the contrary, it is original and immediate, and lies in human nature itself.

The bodhisattva practice of loving-kindness can be a powerful assisting force in our spiritual maturation. Loving-kindness practice—also referred to as *metta* (Pali for "benevolence") or *maitri* (Sanskrit for "friendliness")—helps us show love and compassion to ourselves and everyone. It helps us become assisting forces in the world around us.

In the practice of loving-kindness, we beam these benevolent friendly energies from our inherent Buddha nature first to ourselves, then to others, then to everyone. The practice consists of aspirations we recite aloud or in our minds daily. We are naming and placing an intention for happiness, freedom from fear, liberation, enlightenment, and any other benefits we hope we and others might find. With a heart of loving-kindness, we want any gain or grace in our lives to become continuously beneficial not only to us but to everyone.

We begin aspiring for each of these, one at a time, first for ourselves, then for those close to us, then those toward whom we are neutral (such as a neighbor down the street or the mail carrier). Next our aspirations are directed toward those whom we or society sees as less than or as different from us, then toward those we dislike or who dislike us, and finally toward all beings:

"May I be happy . . ."
"May those I love be happy . . ."
"May those to whom I am neutral be happy . . ."
"May those whom I see as different be happy . . ."
"May those with whom I have difficulty (or who are inimical toward or harmful to me) be happy . . ."
"May all beings be happy . . ."

The practice continues by expressing other aspirations that may be relevant—for example:

"May I be free of fear . . ."
"May those I love be free of fear . . ."
"May those to whom I am neutral be free of fear . . ."
"May those whom I see as different be free of fear . . ."

"May those with whom I have difficulty (or who are inimical toward or harmful to me) be free of fear . . ."
"May all beings be free of fear . . ."

In the traditional loving-kindness practice, there is no mention of those whom we see (or society sees) as different from us, those who are thought to be "less than"—that is, those who are treated as "other." I added this group to my own practice of *metta* as I became more conscious of the racism and myriad other prejudices inherent in myself and in our society. The loving-kindness practice helps free us from biases toward those we may find unimportant, repulsive, untrustworthy, suspect. Our mindset gradually changes as we keep repeating our all-inclusive aspirations for everyone's well-being. With this practice, we begin to live the archetype of the assisting force as we commit ourselves to solidarity with all beings, none excepted. (By contrast, every form of division and separateness cancels our chance to fulfill our luminous human goal to be allies to one another.)

One way of combining psychological work and spiritual practice using what I call "add-metta": You have a feeling-laden interaction with someone, positive or negative in impact. You work on a painful event or traumatic experience from childhood or the recent past. You are triggered by someone and react. After any of these psychological processes, add a short silent loving-kindness practice that sends goodwill to yourself, each of the people in your feeling-event, and all beings who are or have had a similar experience.

Now we see that in the loving-kindness practice we are rewiring our brains in favor of expansive love and letting go of divisiveness. This rewiring happens because we are reversing any sense of isolation and separateness. We are gathering all humans into an equality-awareness. Such a compassionate, joyous embrace widens our own heart. Rainer Maria Rilke, in his *Book of Hours*, wrote, "I live my life in widening circles"—a superb description of the ripple effect of love, the style of *metta*. Here is an image of such circles.

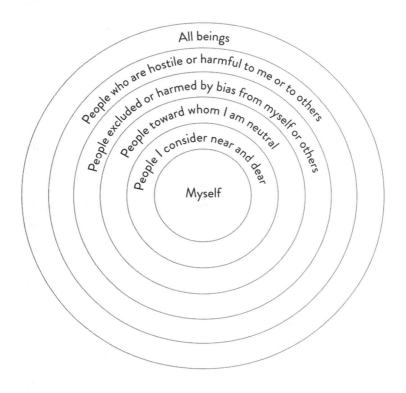

All beings

People who are hostile or harmful to me or to others

People excluded or harmed by bias from myself or others

People toward whom I am neutral

People I consider near and dear

Myself

Felicitously, the same circles form a picture of our own full selves. Our identity is not limited to the center circle but includes all the concentric circles. This inclusivity is how the loving-kindness practice itself shows us that each of us is *more than* an individual. All beings are one with us and expand us—and "with us" here means not beside us but within us. "I am" cannot describe any individual since not one of us is a stand-alone self. (Maybe that is why "I am" is the name God uses, a metaphor for the all-in-everything, the only name that can accurately describe any of us.)

Practicing loving-kindness as in-reach and outreach, unconditional and universal, represents spiritual progress. We are moving from self-love as self-absorption to healthy self-love, the kind of love that expands into a caring for oneself and the wide world too. Such solidarity is how we can trust the effectiveness of a spiritual practice. An ever-expanding love moves us along on our journey toward wholeness, and holding the whole world in our heart is how our own wholeness manifests itself.

This idea about universal love is not only a Buddhist teaching: Flavius Josephus, a Roman Jew in the first century of the Common Era, likewise observed, "I suppose it will become evident someday that the laws in the Torah are meant to lead to a universal love of humanity" (*Contra Apionem* 2:146). He noticed that spirituality was not about fulfilling religious obligations or meriting divine rewards but ultimately and only about showing unlimited love. Let's dare to expand his insight:

- "I suppose it will become evident someday that the laws of a country are meant to lead to a universal love of humanity."
- "I suppose it will become evident someday that the work we do in therapy is meant to lead to a universal love of humanity."
- "I suppose it will become evident someday that our personal relationships are meant to lead us to a universal love of humanity."
- "I suppose it will become evident someday that the Dharma is meant to lead to a universal love of humanity."
- "I suppose it will become evident someday that power is meant to lead to a universal love of humanity."
- "I suppose it will become evident someday that our lifetime here is meant to lead to a universal love of humanity."

What would you add to this list?

We know that our loving-kindness practice is meant to bring more love and compassion into our world. Yet we do not forget that there is a dark side to human nature. We human individuals have deadly inclinations toward division and hatred. Our social-awareness practice is to refrain from acting on these inclinations and to speak up when we see them brutally enacted in society. As individuals we do not have to indulge in them but the potential in all of us is, sadly, undeniable. Our spiritual practices do not eliminate the shadow side of the human collective. But in our commitment to integrity and loving-kindness, we can at least say this: there will never be only love or only peace, but there can be more love than there was before I got here and more peace because I stayed here.

Thanks to the Dharma and to our spirituality we have been let in on the agenda of the universe for ourselves and all humanity. We live in a universe that is so prodigal it gladly gives us myriad opportunities to let go of ego in favor of a universal love. The spiritual practice of loving-kindness thus does not end in our minds. It leads us to become more active in contributing to the welfare of others and the world. We have become especially conscious of the suffering of those who are victims in our society. We show compassion *and* look for ways to act with courage for them in society. We do all this in accord with our individual gifts and personalities.

Who is really practicing loving-kindness? It is our Buddha nature ever alive and awake in us no matter how dead or asleep we may be. Now we see the connection between loving-kindness and becoming bodhisattvas. Since the practice of loving-kindness culminates in a caring compassion toward all beings, that makes bodhisattvahood possible for every one of us. Yes, our practices are preparing us to become caring companions, assisting forces committed to healing our wounded world no matter how wounded we ourselves may be.

In chapter 8 we considered the four qualities of enlightenment: love, compassion, empathic joy, and equanimity. The loving-kindness practice (*metta*) dovetails with the four qualities of enlightenment in the following ways:

- We practice love as all-inclusive friendliness.
- Our friendly response to pain is compassion.
- Our friendly response to others' joy or suffering is feeling it with them.
- Our practice of equanimity means that we are not seduced by what attracts us or repelled by what disgusts us but instead we remain stable and composed in the face of such detours.

A little-known speech from Shakespeare's play *Timon of Athens* offers us a final reminder that compassion for others' suffering really includes active responsiveness to it. We feel compassion and respond to suffering by *doing* something to help alleviate it. In other words, compassion is best practiced by a person committed to being a fully active assisting force:

> Tell them that, to ease them of their griefs,
> Their fears of hostile strokes, their aches, losses,
> Their pangs of love, with other incident throes
> That nature's fragile vessel doth sustain
> In life's uncertain voyage, I will some kindness do them.

OUR CALLING TO LOVING-KINDNESS

In our loving-kindness practice, we love unconditionally not only those who are near and dear to us but all beings. We are individual emissaries of the universe's sacred heart of loving-kindness. Such spiritual affection is our calling, the instinctive drive in our Buddha nature, our opening the love within us.

Throughout this book we have described love as a caring, committed connection—and a connection that is not based on what others do or how they treat us. With this sort of love in our hearts we are no longer seduced by greed, hate, or ignorance—the three poisonings of enlightenment. As self-assisting forces we are saving ourselves from those three poisons. As assisting forces to others we seek the enlightenment of others as we extend unconditional, unreserved, and universal friendliness. And we demonstrate our love through the five A's:

- We are *attending* to others' needs and feelings, not ignoring them.
- We are expressing *affection* toward others, not distancing ourselves from them out of fear of closeness.

- We are *appreciating* others, not taking them for granted—valuing them not demeaning them.
- We are *accepting* others as they are, not rejecting them or attempting to make them over so they will satisfy our ego demands.
- We are *allowing* others to make their own choices, not attempting to manipulate them or control their behavior.

PRACTICE

YES-AND-LOVE AFFIRMATION

I recommend voicing the following aspiration each morning to start the day in a spiritually conscious way. Combining affirmation, aspiration, and dedication, it demonstrates how an affirmation can be an assisting force in our spiritual life, and it affirms our caring, committed connection to all beings—including ourselves, too often omitted.

I say Yes to everything that happens to me today
as an opportunity
to give or receive love and to free myself from fear.
I am thankful for the enduring capacity to love
that has come to me from the sacred heart of the universe.
May everything that happens to me today
open my heart more and more.
May all that I think, say, feel, do, and
am express loving-kindness
toward myself, those close to me, and all beings.
May love be my life purpose, my bliss, my destiny,
my calling,
the richest grace I can receive or give.
And may I always be a compassionate assisting force
toward people who are considered

least or last or who feel alone or lost.
May all of us cocreate
a world of justice, peace, and love.

Now let's ponder this heart-expanding affirmation sentence by sentence.

"I say Yes to everything that happens to me today as an opportunity to give or receive love and to free myself from fear."

We begin by saying yes—that is, we affirm our total acceptance of all that is happening and what will be happening, both in and around us. This hospitality to reality is our unconditional surrender to the givens of life: We are not always in control. Reality does not always match our projections about or expectations of it. We miss so much when we are still quarreling with reality's rules.

When we say yes without reserve, there are actually no longer happenings-just-as-happenings. Now what happens is *more than* a happening; it is an opportunity. In the daily round of challenges, stressful circumstances, and daunting predicaments we are being offered opportunities to give and receive love and to let go of fear—the two central goals of wholesome living. Regarding letting go of fear: we may be afraid of love itself with all its demands on us for full disclosure and total vulnerability. But our yes to what is includes a yes to those scary options. This acceptance turns out to be, fortunately, the first step toward effectively handling our fears.

Our receptive yes builds our trust that what happens is exactly what needs to happen so our story can proceed robustly, so that we can find out what we have to work on, so that we can locate more and more assisting forces, the resources in and around us. In other words, the boldness of our yes has led to our gaining trust in the givens of our own lives as reliable ingredients in our manifestation of wholeness.

"I am thankful for the enduring capacity to love that has come to me from the sacred heart of the universe."

We now feel a sense of abiding gratitude. We realize that our capacity to love has survived countless betrayals and disillusionments, countless bruises and blows. We comprehend that our love is enduring and deathless, no matter how many assailants throw javelins at our hearts. We understand that our love is bigger than our bodymind or our personal feelings. It comes from the heart of the cosmos, our own true heart, enduring and invincible. This heart is sacred, divine—not made of sands that sift away, waters that flow away, flesh that passes away. "Yes" makes love eternal like the cosmos itself.

"May everything that happens to me today open my heart more and more."

Now we feel an aspiration arising in us: we want all the happenings of this day to open our capacities to love. Happenings have now become not only opportunities but keys. We become open to all that is or will be unfolding in our life today. This opening is the immediate result, and gift, that arises from our recognition of a love in us that just can't die.

"May all that I think, say, feel, do, and am express loving-kindness toward myself, those close to me, and all beings."

We are now moved to dedicate everything about us on this day to the cultivation of loving-kindness. Our yes to happenings as opportunities has become yes to the central opportunity: to practice loving-kindness not only toward ourselves but toward everyone.

"May love be my life purpose, my bliss, my destiny, my calling, the richest grace I can receive or give."

Now we aspire that love become conscious in us as an animating purpose, a joy, a life purpose, a calling, and especially a grace. We trust an evolutionary impulse in us to show itself everywhere and to everyone without reserve or boundary.

"And may I always be a compassionate assisting force toward people who are considered least or last or who feel alone or lost."

Finally, we ask to be assisting forces especially to those who need us most, the excluded, those considered by some members and policies of society to be the least and last. Likewise, we feel compassion for the lonesome, the lost—what sometimes we have experienced on our own life path. Thus our compassion easily flowers on this terrain of loving-kindness. And the budding all began with a yes.

We now join with all beings and dedicate ourselves to our universal calling to create together a world of justice, peace, and love.

When we sincerely intend a day of yes and love, we draw the assisting forces to us. They include all those from whom we learned how to love. We invite them to act through us. These are the spiritual allies we have admired, reverenced, and imitated over the years. They lived out the yes-and-love practice. When we live it too, even in small ways, we are full-fledged assisting forces like them. After all, what are we here for if not to give every one of these saints and bodhisattvas, every holy spirit, every helpful ancestor, one more chance to have a lifetime, this time with our body and name? To put it in verse:

What have we ever,
More or better,
Than our life together?

EPILOGUE THE POWER OF YES

Our lives are an unconditional yes to reality when we follow pathways like these:

- We live in the here and now and see it mindfully—that is, openly and without judgment, impartially, and not afraid of what we are facing in the moment or of what next may happen. We welcome all that happens to us with an unreserved hospitality.
- We unconditionally accept the givens of life: things change and end, life is not always fair, our plans may fall through, pain is part of everyone's life, people may not be loving and loyal toward us all the time.

A yes to the givens of life is not resignation to them. Indeed, the yes of acceptance is too active an experience to be a noun. True accepting is more like accommodating our debating partner's presentation of ideas—even if our response includes some anger. It is still acceptance, because we are willing to open to whatever is coming our way and is beyond our control—whether or not we agree with it or like it.

With an unconditional dedication to life as it is, we notice that we no longer ask "Why?" We only say, "Yes, now what?" This transition from why to yes is the threshold into and the apex of spiritual maturity.

Jung, in his commentary on *The Secret of the Golden Flower,* wrote: "The art of letting things happen, action through non-action, letting go of oneself, as taught by Meister Eckhart, became for me the key opening the door to the way." We have all heard the expression about life being what happens while we are making other plans. When we remember how we thought our life would go and compare it to how it has actually been, we marvel at how great a gap can open between concrete reality and our imagined version of our story. Life itself turns out to be the assisting force that helps us distinguish fantasy from reality, and it all begins with our song of yes.

As for myself as I come to the end of this book:

I am thankful for the many assisting forces in my life so far.
May I welcome the assisting forces soon to arrive.
May I always be an assisting force to others.

ABOUT THE AUTHOR

DAVID RICHO, PHD, is a psychotherapist, writer, and workshop leader. He has taught at a variety of places including Esalen, Spirit Rock Retreat Center, San Francisco Zen Center, and San Damiano Retreat Center. He shares his time between Santa Barbara and San Francisco, California. Dave combines psychological and spiritual perspectives in his work. His website is davericho.com.

BOOKS AND AUDIO BY DAVID RICHO

How to Be an Adult: A Handbook on Psychological and Spiritual Integration (Paulist Press, 1991)

Shadow Dance: Liberating the Power and Creativity of Your Dark Side (Shambhala Publications, 1999)

The Five Things We Cannot Change and the Happiness We Find by Embracing Them (Shambhala Publications, 2005)

The Power of Coincidence: How Life Shows Us What We Need to Know (Shambhala Publications, 2007)

The Sacred Heart of the World: Restoring Mystical Devotion to Our Spiritual Life (Paulist Press, 2007)

Making Love Last: How to Sustain Intimacy and Nurture Connection (audiobook; Shambhala Publications, 2008)

When the Past Is Present: Healing the Emotional Wounds That Sabotage Our Relationships (Shambhala Publications, 2008)

Being True to Life: Poetic Paths to Personal Growth (Shambhala Publications, 2009)

Daring to Trust: Opening Ourselves to Real Love and Intimacy (Shambhala Publications, 2010)

How to Be an Adult in Faith and Spirituality (Paulist Press, 2011)

Coming Home to Who You Are: Discovering Your Natural Capacity for Love, Integrity, and Compassion (Shambhala Publications, 2011)

Embracing the Shadow: Discovering The Hidden Riches in Our Relationships (set of four CDs; Shambhala Publications, 2013)

How to Be an Adult in Love: Letting Love in Safely and Showing It Recklessly (Shambhala Publications, 2013)

The Power of Grace: Recognizing Unexpected Gifts on Our Path (Shambhala Publications, 2014)

When Catholic Means Cosmic: Opening to a Big-Minded, Big-Hearted Faith (Paulist Press, 2015)

You Are Not What You Think: The Egoless Path to Self-Esteem and Generous Love (Shambhala Publications, 2015)

When Mary Becomes Cosmic: A Jungian and Mystical Path to the Divine Feminine (Paulist Press, 2016)

The Five Longings: What We've Always Wanted and Already Have (Shambhala Publications, 2017)

Everything Ablaze: Meditating on the Mystical Vision of Teilhard de Chardin (Paulist Press, 2017)

Five True Things: A Little Guide to Embracing Life's Big Challenges (Shambhala Publications, 2019)

Triggers: How We Can Stop Reacting and Start Healing (Shambhala Publications, 2019)

Wholeness and Holiness: How to Be Sane, Spiritual, and Saintly (Orbis, 2020)

How to Be an Adult in Relationships: The Five Keys to Mindful Loving (revised edition; Shambhala Publications, 2021)

Ready: How to Know When to Go and When to Stay
(Shambhala Publications, 2022)

*When Love Meets Fear: How to Become Defense-less and
Resource-full* (revised edition; Paulist Press, 2022)

*To Thine Own Self Be True: Shakespeare as Therapist and
Spiritual Guide* (Paulist Press, 2023)